A testimony of Go[...]
in the wilc[...]

ESCAPED

As a bird from the snare

HANNAH
NIGHTINGALE

Dedication

To my pastor and his wife

Entrusted to walk the whole way through this wilderness journey with me. Thank you for the prayers that held me up and your steadfast faith in God and His Word alone. Your faith and imparting of God's Word became a lamp, held out before me, to guide each of my steps along a treacherous path. Whilst never forced to tread this path, the call of God and a yearning to draw nearer to Him could never be forsaken. You also both know there are no easy shortcuts to knowing Christ and have set your faces like flint towards the upward call. Yet what treasures and delights we have discovered en-route in those darkest of places. Thank you for being the companions who sought out those riches with me.

I will give you the treasures of darkness and hidden riches of secret places, that you may know that I, the LORD, who call you by your name, am the God of Israel.

Isaiah 45:3

Foreword

It is a privilege to be asked to write a Foreword to this book. It describes the author's personal journey with the Lord through a wilderness of perplexity, hardship and anguish of soul, in which she held fast to the faithfulness of God in what often seemed the most unlikely of circumstances.

I cannot remember reading a book which glorifies the Lord more greatly in its account of determination, in the midst of difficulties that often appeared insurmountable, to trust in the Lord's utter faithfulness to overcome every obstacle and provide every need. Hannah's walk was often one of hardship and tears, but her commitment to God and her determination to follow Him no matter how hard the path, breathes through every page of her testimony. His faithfulness to her is matched by her faithfulness to trust and obey Him, often in the darkness of pain, confusion and uncertainty.

The way of the wilderness is a path on which all true disciples of the Lord Jesus are called to walk in some measure. It is the path upon which Moses was called to lead the Israelites out of slavery in Egypt; and its lessons are spelt out in Deuteronomy 8 – the testing of obedience, together with the humbling, which results from experiencing utter helplessness apart from the Lord's intervention and provision. This same path was the experience of the Lord Jesus following His baptism in Jordan, and of Paul during his years in Arabia (Galatians 1:17-18).

It is a path on which the doubts and difficulties are such that the disciple is frequently tempted to turn back. Hannah Nightingale, however, has such trust in the Lord that she set her face like flint in every situation of difficulty and seeming impossibility; and her walk has resulted in a testimony of the faithfulness of God and a beautiful account of His dealings that have purified His servant and strengthened her for the days ahead. It is a joy to be able to commend her book to His people.

David Noakes
Bible teacher and adviser to Issachar Ministries

Endorsement

Abusive relationships are used by the enemy to steal, kill and destroy. As a former victim of an abusive husband, the wounds are deep, yet unseen. So what does life to the full (John 10:10b) look like for one who is in an abusive marriage?

In this book you will find described a life seeking and finding hope in the Lord. Composed with deep insight, it presents an unbiased account that honours God, with His wisdom flowing through each page. This will speak to many – not only to those in a similar situation, but also to those pastorally called to support people in abusive situations.

Incredibly well written, a resource and voice in an area where there are disproportionately few resources available and even fewer sermons, despite the sad reality that abuse lies hidden in many 'Christian' marriages. May the Lord guide each of us to His truth on the subjects of abuse, marriage and divorce – not the views of religion, legalism or hyper-grace. I hope this goes some way in exposing what should no longer remain hidden and empower many more to tell their story.

Dr Elene Haralambous
Survivor of marital abuse, set free and healed by Jesus Christ

Acknowledgements

Special thanks to:

All at Living Stones Fellowship – I could not have produced this book without your prayers, practical support and generosity. Thank you. The faith you displayed in doing this amazes me. What a precious family God has given me in you all. Our love for one another will be our strength for the days ahead.

Andy Economides (and Soteria Trust) – for your generosity and much-needed advice. Thank you for the giving of your time. Your book had a role to play in my journey to freedom, essentially leading to the writing of this book. May it go on to touch many more lives for God's glory.

Chris Wickland – for all the support, wisdom and kindness you have shown me, all wrapped up in good humour. Living Word Fellowship has made me feel welcome on the very special 'Prayer Farm' and it has been a privilege to be involved in that work. The Lord has big plans there.

David Noakes – a humble fore-runner of the wilderness experience. It has been a blessing to have had the opportunity to glean your wisdom and enjoy fellowship through the sharing of our testimonies of God's faithfulness in our lives. Keep pressing on into what God still has for you to do, and it will inspire me to do the same! You are nearly home.

Those who came alongside me in prayer at any time during this four-year period – I fear if I attempt to name you all, I may accidentally miss someone. You know who you are. Thank you for playing your part. By investing into me, you invested into this story and its eternal purposes. I am so grateful for each one of you. Please keep coming alongside the broken and the weak, for you don't know what impact it will have for God's kingdom.

Contents

Preface

These are the journeys of the children of Israel, who went out of the land of Egypt by their armies under the hand of Moses and Aaron. Now Moses wrote down the starting points of their journeys at the command of the LORD. And these are their journeys according to their starting points.

Numbers 33:1-2

These two verses, given to me by the Lord, are the reason for this book. Simply put, God wanted me to write down the testimony of a child of God's journey out of bondage (Egypt), under the mighty hand of her leader. I am the child of God in this story and my leader, Jesus Christ. I don't want to presume how this will minister to you, or that it will at all, only that this story belongs to God; He wrote it and entrusted me to walk it. Now, in obedience to His command, I testify of it and commit it back to Him to use as He wills. May He receive all the praise and glory.

Our soul has escaped as a bird from the snare of the fowlers; the snare is broken, and we have escaped.

Psalm 124:7

Introduction

Michael and I married in 2010. He had not been a Christian long yet he exhibited a boldness, zealousness and spirituality that attracted me to him. Previous generations of his family had been travellers and there remained an essence of this lifestyle among them still. Many of Michael's family members are believed to have come to saving faith at a Christian meeting after his grandma was healed from deafness in one ear. Michael was nine years old at the time. The rest of his wider family (of which there were many) remained rebellious. In his latter teenage years Michael was frequently getting into trouble – usually stealing and getting into fights. However, he did make a commitment to the Lord in his twenties, resulting in the curtailing of this negative lifestyle.

In the midst of Michael's devotion and zeal for reading scripture there would be episodes of concerning behaviour – jealousy, control, anger, aggression and aversion to fellowship to name a few. He was able to acknowledge some of this and I concluded at the time that allowance was needed for the 'sanctification process'. There were times he would be too harsh in attempting to correct me over certain things he had misjudged. His language towards me could be abusive and he was prone to irrationality and overreacting, resulting in incidents of violence. This mainly involved damaging property and various items in my presence, but there were also a few occasions I was roughly handled and one occurrence of a more severe physical incident towards me. I didn't share this with anyone as I felt a loyalty towards Michael still. He had also been unfaithful in the marriage on one occasion. He displayed sincere remorse, appearing repentant, so I chose to forgive him and preserve the marriage. I'd bargained with God that if I forgave then surely God would not allow the same hurt and sin against me again. Needless to say, God told me that my forgiveness was to have no conditions attached to it and that I should forgive Michael knowing that the same trespass could be perpetrated against me again. The Lord gave me grace and refined me through all of these trials.

Over the next few years Michael's Christian faith acted as a restraint against certain behaviours and violent actions, though there always remained a threat of re-emergence. He struggled with patterns of giving up smoking then starting again and went through periods of not attending church, believing he needed to give up smoking first. There was a noticeable lack of steadfastness in his walk with the Lord and I am unsure what lasting fruit there was. We did pray together during his seasons of 'closeness' to God and he would have spells of intense Bible study, which would then lapse. Due to his impersistent nature and double-mindedness I was always the main breadwinner. His jobs and plans for work never lasted long before he was seeking out another idea. Michael tended to prioritise time with his brother, preferring to spend his time on the land the family owned rather than at home. After years of contending this, I learned to accept it rather than let bitterness triumph. This way, when I did have time with him, we tended to get along fine. The negatives didn't always dominate and, on the whole, Michael was a good father and capable of showing me love and kindness. I loved him, considering him a friend as well as a husband.

Blessed are those who mourn,
for they shall be comforted.

Matthew 5:4

1.

A Time To Mourn

Unexpectedly pregnant with our second child

My story starts in November 2019 – nine and half years into my marriage to Michael. This month, we moved house with our daughter, aged five at the time. In the December, Michael lost his grandad to cancer. They had been very close and he spent time at his bedside ministering the Word to him before his final breath.

We found out after this that I was unexpectedly pregnant with our second child, and Michael accompanied me, in the February, to the first scan at twelve weeks gestation. I remember excitedly exclaiming I could see our baby on the monitor before it was very swiftly turned away from me, accompanied by silence – the kind of silence where you could hear a pin drop. I was told the baby's heartbeat had stopped at around eleven weeks old. The tears immediately spilled as Michael came over to console me. I asked where the toilets were and, when alone with God, all I could say to Him was, *'I don't understand, but I trust You. I need You now.'*

We were shown out by the back door of the hospital to avoid walking past the jubilant faces of expectant mothers in the waiting room. I carried our dead baby inside me for the next two to three weeks not knowing if or when I would miscarry, what this would be like or where I'd be when it happened. No miscarriage took place but during this time I still felt pregnant and was experiencing the same symptoms as I had been throughout the pregnancy. Another scan was booked with the intention to surgically remove the baby.

A sweetness to behold within the comfort of the Lord

During this time Michael had believed the Lord could and would miraculously restart our baby's heartbeat. Sadly, at the next scan there was still no heartbeat. Michael was angry. But God had never given us a Word that He would do this.

I was shown on the screen that our baby was still comfortably sitting within the lining of the womb where she'd died. I began wondering if I'd done something to cause this life to just stop in me. *What had I been doing around eleven weeks? Had I been eating badly or not enough? Had I been stressed or overworked?* These questions were unhelpful and I knew deep down I was not to blame. Although full of sadness, the Lord drew very close to me during the grieving period, giving me His peace. There was such a sweetness to behold within the comfort of the Lord. I knew He was with me and my soul was secure with Him.

Hard times are coming . . .

I would not usually have named a baby so early on in pregnancy but I had sensed I was having a girl and was sure of this to the extent I gave her the name Abigail. After the loss and during a time of prayer, the Lord graciously revealed to a friend that myself and my daughter, Rebecca, had both lost sisters (I'd lost a twin sister as a baby). With my friend having no prior knowledge that I'd believed the baby had been female, this proved to be a comforting confirmation from the Lord.

Our five-year-old daughter kept asking me why God had taken the baby. One time I replied that I didn't know, only that I had a peace about it, but if she wanted she could ask God and He may share the reason with her. No sooner had I finished speaking than she said, '*Oh, He just said it's because hard times are coming and He didn't want the baby to be scared.*' This took me aback as I knew this had not come from her. She was only five and didn't use this kind of language, nor could she have made it up. I was about to find out how true those words were.

For You formed my inward parts; You covered me in my mother's womb. I will praise You, for I am fearfully and wonderfully made; marvellous are Your works.

Psalm 139:13-14

2.

The Abortion Reality

Baby cut to pieces and suctioned out

Processing the loss of my baby brought an unexpected issue to light. I recalled being made to wait in a hospital room for some time, sitting facing a large poster with the words *Thinking of having an abortion?* on it. A rather insensitive touch for someone whose baby had been very much loved and wanted. Looking back, I realised I had been dealt with by the same professionals who performed abortions. The same hands that undertook my procedure, known as 'surgical management of miscarriage', would have perhaps undertaken 'surgical abortions' that day. It was the same procedure, the only difference being that in a surgical abortion, the baby is very much alive when the 'sharp tipped hollow tube is inserted and the baby cut to pieces and suctioned out of their mother's womb into a glass cannister'.[1]

My heart grieved for these babies

No doubt there would be an emptiness engulfing these women after this procedure. Had they seen a scan picture of their beautifully forming son or daughter before the procedure, like I had? Had they seen on screen the flickering of their baby's heartbeat, which had begun beating from three weeks? Or did they believe that a clump of cells was simply being removed and it was a 'pregnancy' being ended, not their son's or daughter's life? Some perhaps would recognise a pricking on their conscience or a persistent guilt, whilst others would bury that guilt and shame under the repeated narrative, *It's my body, my choice,* until the hardening of their hearts would make way for self-deception to settle. Did they know they

---
1   Centre for Bio-Ethical Reform UK (CBRUK).

could be released and healed by the acknowledgement and repentance of this sin? I'd heard it said that abortion does not prevent a woman becoming a mother. Instead, she becomes the mother to a dead baby. My heart grieved for these babies and also for those mothers and fathers who would need healing afterwards. How much more does God's heart grieve for those He has wonderfully formed, having already planned out their lives?

We can no longer claim ignorance

Abortion, the taking of a human life, promoted as 'healthcare' and advertised by the poster I had to stare at, was an issue the Lord had needed to open my eyes to. Once our eyes are open, we can no longer claim ignorance and therefore we are accountable for what we do or don't do as a result. It was that year, 2020, God was going to connect me with two women to start regularly praying about this issue, which has seen the killing of an estimated 10 million babies (currently 600 a day) in the UK since the 1967 Abortion Act.[2]

Prayer soon led to action as I joined pro-life displays, in which we would stand in public with two display boards: one showing an eight-week foetus; the other showing the graphic image of an aborted eight-week foetus, some of their body parts recognisable in the image. We engaged with the public in many fruitful conversations, praying with many. However, on occasions we would be subjected to irate women (and occasionally men) who would hurl abuse in our faces. Others took a more passive-aggressive approach in calling the police or, as it happened on one occasion, parking a vehicle illegally in front of the displays. I had to develop thick skin, and quickly, but every so often one of the enemy's fiery darts would make contact. This was where the battle was at. The Lord reminded me that the woman who told me directly I was an attention-seeker . . . was hurting. The lady who called me a child-abuser . . . was hurting. The woman, standing scowling at us from her window, stationary for one and a half hours . . . was hurting. I'd said nothing to them . . . just two pictures had confronted them with sin.

---

2   CBRUK statistics. See page 191 for more abortion statistics.

Sin will not remain buried forever and its exposure now was better than exposure at a time when it would be too late to repent.

It was this exposure of sin that was causing the emotional, irrational and angry responses around us. Deep down people knew the images they were looking at were human lives. How long had those who had partaken in abortion carried such guilt and pain? Where was NHS healthcare for them now? I hadn't seen any posters advertising healing after abortion. I took no pleasure or joy in the uncovering of sin in people's lives. I had fallen short many times and knew only too well the aftermath of guilt and shame. Yet, this is what it is to truly love people. By confronting them with this sin, and bringing them to an acknowledgement that we are sinners, an answer of hope could be given: Jesus Christ, the only sacrifice made for our sins so that we could be completely forgiven and set free from the wages of sin – death.

He is despised and rejected by men,
a Man of sorrows and acquainted with grief.
And we hid, as it were, our faces from Him;
He was despised, and we did not esteem Him.

Isaiah 53:3

3.

Despised And Rejected

Shadows of his old self were emerging

Covid restrictions began in March 2020. Michael had to stop most of his work but I continued working, remaining still as the breadwinner. During this time he was rebellious towards the government rules and started to become engrossed with media coverage of President Trump. He became paranoid about the Covid vaccine, fuelled by programmes he would frequently watch with his dad. He would become very animated over these topics and fearful over Rebecca, relaying (in front of her) that authorities could come and take her away or the school could force the vaccine into her. Whilst I, too, had chosen not to take the vaccine, I had a peace about my decision without getting caught up in the various arguments. He, on the other hand, appeared unsettled and consumed by these media outlets with fear appearing to be the driving force behind his behaviour. Shadows of his old self were emerging and I felt led to message some trusted believers in the Lord to ask for their prayers for him.

Increasingly distant

As I drew closer in my walk with the Lord, Michael became increasingly distant. He was no longer interested if I shared spiritual things with him and I would struggle with the forceful, oppressive and intimidating way in which he expressed his views. His anger also became more apparent. He rejected offers to pray things through with me – I felt there was a real exposure taking place. He began to go to places only inviting Rebecca to go with him, spending little time at home and choosing to sleep on the sofa, stating it was better for his back. I can remember the sadness and pain I experienced during many nights where I would clutch my Bible and cry myself to sleep. I would wonder what I had done and asked the Lord why I felt ostracised, rejected and despised. Despite the sorrow, I started to enjoy my time alone with the Lord and would retreat to the bedroom. This way I could avoid Michael's difficult behaviour and domineering opinions. I desired instead to fellowship with the Lord – He was my safe place: *'The eternal God is your refuge, and underneath are the everlasting arms'* (Deuteronomy 33:27).

You are my hiding place;
You shall preserve me from trouble;
You shall surround me with songs of deliverance.
Selah

Psalm 32:7

4.

Songs In The Night

Wake up, be sober and strengthen what remains

In the same year (2020), I began to receive songs from the Lord. In the midst of all that was going on, the songs ministered to me as I focused my thoughts on scripture. They became an outlet and expression of God's Holy Spirit in me during a season of oppression within the home. The songs allowed entry to a safe place where my spirit and the Lord's could commune and there was sometimes a prophetic message expressed through them.

Although I considered my singing as weak and inconsistent, with my piano playing limited, the pull from the Holy Spirit to write and share these songs became stronger and stronger. To keep resisting and protesting would have been disobedient to the Lord's call, so in the end I had to surrender. I'd taken two days to pluck up the courage to message a contact called Lydia, who I knew to be musically talented, asking her if she would help with the first song. She accepted before even hearing it (which I thought very risky) and sang, played the violin and recorded it for me. This song spoke of the church needing to wake up, be sober and strengthen what remains, for the day of the Lord is near.

An anointing was given

Retrospectively, God had another purpose – it was to be the start of a valuable friendship, proving significant for the days ahead. Lydia told me she looked forward to hearing further songs of mine. I brushed this off, stating adamantly this song was a one-off. It turned out not to be a 'throw away' comment from her. True to her words, along came a second song. God placed over me an indescribable and overwhelming sense of His love and presence. It seemed to remain and rest over me for approximately three days, during which time I believe an anointing was given. Enveloped in His presence, I knew I couldn't get away with not singing this next one myself.

I learnt to succumb more quickly to these Holy Spirit compulsions, realising that breaking out of my comfort zone was necessary for my spiritual growth. I'd like to say my singing and playing immediately improved from this point of apparent anointing – but it didn't. Yet somehow, God enabled me to 'wing it' by His grace and I found ways of recording vocals, even just a line at a time, which certainly helped reduce embarrassment when, by His spirit, I was compelled to share the song recordings that kept coming.

He improved the 'wrapping' of this gift

Somehow, gradually over time, my playing skill improved and my voice strengthened, becoming more consistently in tune. I was sure any lack of ability never really mattered to the Lord as it was more about conveying His message through the songs. Despite my efforts of self-preservation, by God's mercy and kindness He improved the 'wrapping' of this gift, so that more people might receive it and, upon opening, be ministered to. So often man looks at the outward appearance and, if impressed by this, comes to the conclusion that there is an anointing inside, but sadly there are many beautifully wrapped presents that lack any substance when opened. By taking something I had no natural confidence in, the Lord was able to increase my dependency upon Him, whilst displaying His strength and Spirit through my weakness and inability. This ensured He received all the glory.

A snare for self-promotion and time wasting

I was encouraged by Lydia to set up a YouTube channel, which I indignantly dismissed. I wasn't a fan of YouTube or Facebook, seeing these social media platforms as a snare for self-promotion and time wasting. I didn't want attention and I felt there would be a vulnerability I wasn't ready for in exposing myself in this way. Of course, it should never really have been about me at all. One evening, just after putting Rebecca to bed, I started a time of prayer with the Lord. I remember asking Him specifically, *'Lord, is there something I'm doing that I shouldn't be, or anything I'm not doing that I should be, for me to move forward with you?'*

God must have liked that prayer because just after I'd prayed that, Rebecca called me from her bedroom. Initially I was agitated at my prayer time being interrupted but her little voice called down to me, *'Mummy, I've got something important to tell you.'* I knew then in my spirit, what she was about to say would relate to the question I'd just asked in prayer. I went up to see what was worthy of beckoning me back upstairs at a time when she should be going to sleep. She simply said to me, *'Mummy, I was thinking about* Jesus of Nazareth. *John the Baptist was making a lot of noise in prison, wasn't he?'* We had been watching the film *Jesus of Nazareth* that evening and she'd clearly been pondering over it in her head with this statement being her important message to tell me. In the film, they certainly had depicted John the Baptist as making a lot of noise from the prison cell.

'More noise' for Him

I knew the Lord wanted me to make 'more noise' for Him and that the songs containing His truths were also important for preparing the church, His bride, for the return of the bridegroom, Jesus. So rather tentatively I set up my YouTube channel, giving it a fitting name to what had been revealed to me. Just so Lydia didn't think she'd won on this one, I refused to promote anything, believing God could direct people to it if He wanted. Probably unlike anyone else that has a YouTube channel, I kept my eye on the number of views hoping it would remain low to save exposure of my inability!

God was gracious to surround me with those in my fellowship who would encourage me in the gift God had given me. I was touched by their kindness and nurturing of that which still needed cultivating. I think discouragement at this early stage could have had a detrimental effect and so I am always mindful to try and recognise in others how the Lord is growing their gifts, that I may give them the same encouragement and kindness I received.

Rebecca's declaration regarding the 'noisy John the Baptist' from within prison served as a picture to me of how it is possible to be a voice for Jesus from a place of affliction and those circumstances that imprison us:

Remember that Jesus Christ, of the seed of David, was raised from the dead according to my gospel, for which I suffer trouble as an evildoer, even to the point of chains; but the word of God is not chained.

2 Timothy 2:8-9

*For I think that God has displayed us, the apostles, last,
as men condemned to death; for we have been made a
spectacle to the world, both to angels and to men.
We are fools for Christ's sake, but you are wise in Christ!*

1 Corinthians 4:9-10

5.

Fools For Christ

I'd hated drama at school

God's promptings took on an even more bold direction for me when it came to some of the song videos. I remember being in bed awake at about 1am one night, completely inspired and convinced that one song video required me to put on my wedding dress. I was to smear mud over it as a visual depiction of the state of the church as the bride of Christ. Needless to say, by morning, when sanity of mind was more tangible, I was less enthusiastic about this but still felt it was something the Lord would have me do.

I'd hated drama at school, being especially shy and self-conscious. I shuddered as I recalled my drama teacher. 'Mrs A' we called her; an American lady, overly exuberant, at least for my English blood. Sure, she had been fun outside the classroom but her idea of 'fun' within lessons was to pick at random someone to come to the front of the class and stand before everyone. On their own they would have to act out, off-the-cuff, a scene she would give them. I'd been picked once. A polite *'No thank you'* fell on deaf ears as I was swiftly summoned to use the prop telephone. My directive? To receive a call from an imaginary boyfriend who would dump me. *Oh joy. A part I'd always dreamed of.*

Before I had time to process this, *'GO!'* was screeched at me. I hesitantly went to pick up the phone opting not to impersonate a ring tone, so Mrs A, wasting no time in finding herself a part, self-assuredly became the 'bring-bring' of the telephone. It was downhill from there. I stood like a rabbit in the headlights and painfully muffled the odd response word in-between prolonged silences, making out the 'boyfriend' on the other end of the phoneline was doing all the talking! Far too embarrassed and hating the attention, I brought this non-starter of a performance to a swift end, deciding I'd just hang up on him. I couldn't even make that very dramatic as I gently placed the receiver back down. Job done.

To say my audience were less than enthralled would be an understatement. Mrs A was not impressed at my insipid portrayal of what could have been an entertaining scene. However, it worked in my favour as I don't remember being picked on again; she had clearly determined I possessed no hidden talent waiting to be discovered when it came to acting.

I can only conclude, then, that God was at work when I found myself standing in the middle of a field in a wedding dress looking particularly dishevelled and dirty. It was far from glamourous. I'd had a real dilemma of how I was to walk to this field without alerting attention to myself and looking odd to passers-by, struggling to find a coat long enough to cover the dress. I'd heard it said there are shoes for every occasion but I managed to debunk that theory that day. So, resigned to just looking weird, I departed the house in a dress hopelessly and unsuccessfully concealed by a long coat, having slipped on a comfortable pair of trainers.

The need to redeem the time

Lydia, enlisted as my camera woman, had endured an interesting introduction to our friendship. Her earliest memory of meeting me, which she doesn't let me forget, was when I had an unfortunate bout of food poisoning whilst driving; the sudden queasiness forcing a swift pulling over on the motorway, requiring her to take over the wheel. Following this, I filled up her email inbox with some pitiful singing recordings, sent one line at a time, which undoubtedly stretched her skills to the limit, having the job of transforming them into something half presentable.

Now, perhaps only the fourth occasion we'd met up, she said she'd never laughed so much filming me in this field. She got to know me really well in a very short space of time, with our friendship bypassing the usual introductory phase of conventional and ordinary interactions. We tended to get down to business, supporting one another in the stewarding of what God had entrusted us with. We recognised the need to redeem the time, especially having sensed the heavy darkness encroaching the world. Despite these occasions where I was probably an embarrassment to her, she remained a faithful friend, discerning the potential beyond what, to the natural eye, looked unrefined and rough around the edges.

The church's rejection and desertion of Christ

While we were out filming, we did come across passers-by (and a horse rider) but, being British, politeness won over curiosity or concern and no one questioned why a bride would be out in a field covered in mud looking distressed. I'm not sure if I found that more relieving or disconcerting.

In a moment of sobriety, however, I thought of Ezekiel and the visual messages he was required to act out to communicate God's voice to His people. It seemed often the one delivering the message has to *become* the message and the story themselves. It hadn't escaped my notice that here I was as a rejected spouse, depicting something of the church's rejection and desertion of Christ. This was a role the Lord was going to have me further 'act out' in my life through events yet to unfold. A performance of rejection that would satisfy even Mrs A.

Now the Spirit expressly says that in latter times some will depart from the faith, giving heed to deceiving spirits and doctrines of demons, speaking lies in hypocrisy, having their own conscience seared with a hot iron.

1 Timothy 4:1-2

6.

As Day Hands Over To The Night

I'd be living like I was treading on egg shells

On Christmas Eve 2020, I received a text message from Michael to say that he was leaving and that his anxiety had been bad. He stated he'd been unsettled and lacking peace due to our relationship because, according to him, I dishonoured him and was disobedient. His messages were full of accusation and criticism about menial things that he had never discussed properly with me. For example, citing one occasion he did not like what I'd given Rebecca for dinner and on another occasion had an issue with me leaving the laptop charger plugged in at the wall, unattached to the laptop, with the switch on. He saw this as a big safety issue.

Having been married to Michael for ten years now, I had become accustomed to most of his expectations and requirements of me but found them burdensome. Where they were not always logical or reflective of moral standards, I couldn't always remember to keep them and so at times I'd be living like I was treading on egg shells, anxious to not provoke and arouse anger from him. He did not want to discuss or resolve anything, having formed an impression of me that was untrue. He had made up his mind. He said he had been seeking God, going on walks and praying. He said that when he prayed about separation the anxiety left him and he had peace. I do not believe this peace came from God and tried to encourage him to *'test the spirits'* (1 John 4:1).

Little reasoning could touch him

It shocked me knowing that his heart had turned against me in this way and that little reasoning could touch him. The husband that had been capable of loving me and being my friend was no longer there. He had set himself up as my enemy having formed the belief, or having been deceived into believing, that I was the cause of his problems. There was a tense and heightened spiritual atmosphere in the house in the months that followed. Strangely, I could sense the presence of demons in the home, which made me feel jumpy and like I was being watched. I knew I had stepped into a spiritual battle and they were trying to intimidate me. I knew in my spirit that the Lord had not permitted them to come too close, keeping them at a distance. God gave me such joy as I praised and prayed in tongues, which also acted as a deterrent to the enemy. I knew that the Lord had required me to walk through this valley and that He indeed was with me. After all, I had been warned through our daughter that hard times were coming.

****

You lead me down into the valley
As day hands over to the night
Already there's a trodden path before me
And my eyes fix on Your light.

The accuser waits by in the shadows
The name I bear stops him drawing near
The lies and whispers will very soon drown out
As my praises reach his ear

**So I'll take along this love song
For however long it takes
And then forever more
For You're the faithful One
To whom I belong
My beloved I do adore**

Whilst I know not the length of this valley
Nor the number of each wound and sore
Once I'm through you'll smell no fire on me
And my clothes whiter than before.

Let sleeping souls that lie in this valley
Wake as I pass Your light by them
Would a testimony flow from this broken vessel
To lead out of darkness again.

In this world there will be tribulation
But You have overcome
We're more than conquerors in You

Peace like a river
In this valley
I've found Your river
In this valley.

****

LYRICS FROM 'THIS VALLEY'
2020 SONG BY HANNAH

Now then, we are ambassadors for Christ, as though God were pleading through us: we implore you on Christ's behalf, be reconciled to God. For He made Him who knew no sin to be sin for us, that we might become the righteousness of God in Him.

2 Corinthians 5:20-21

7.

Ambassador For Christ

He had been messaging another woman

T he Lord required me to act blamelessly towards Michael, showing all grace, forgiveness and blessing him when he would act harshly or accuse me. The accusations came verbally and via messages, this becoming more of a regular pattern now. I didn't always get it right but the Lord was training me in His ways. I had to overcome the flesh and emotions so that neither would hinder the waging of this war. I was aware through a friend that he had been messaging another woman from Ireland on Facebook, yet the Lord still gave me faith to contend for the marriage.

My body, my rights, my service and unconditional love were to be laid before him

Knowing of this betrayal, I was surprised when the Lord required me to make an appeal to Michael prior to his leaving. God taught me through the narratives of Esther and Abigail about the godly way a woman is to appeal to a man who is intent on taking the wrong course of action. Esther appealed to King Xerxes to spare the life of the Jews and Abigail appealed to David not to attack her husband and their household. I asked God specifically what I was to offer to Michael – *Should I cook him a meal? Give a gift?* The response was unequivocal – *You are to offer all of yourself, nothing held back. Fully yielded and submissive.* I was to freely offer to Michael all that I was without condition or demand for anything in return. My body, my rights, my service and unconditional love were to be laid before him. I had to ask the Lord if he knew how Michael had treated me and all he had done against me. Of course the Lord knew, but He needed my obedience and sacrifice in this. So I fasted and prepared myself. The Lord's request of me spoke of Jesus humbly stooping low from great heights, down into this dark world in order to reach us in our rebellion and rescue us from our sin. The forsaking of any rights and my pride, stooping low to reach Michael, seemed to be God's requirement of me at this time. I was hopeful that because the Lord wanted me to do this, it would have a positive outcome.

I really had to battle self-pity and depression

However, Michael rejected me, stating it was too late. He appeared proud and hard-hearted that evening. I'd offered everything to him unconditionally, demanding nothing in return, so that all I had hold of was the Lord. It seemed, therefore, it was my devotion to the Lord and the Lord Himself he was actually rejecting. If Michael could not be the one sitting on the throne in our home (as opposed to Christ), then it appeared he no longer wanted to remain in the home.

I felt such pain that evening, for the Lord and myself. We had been rejected after everything we had done for him and given to him. I struggled immensely after this — having lost a baby and now a husband, knowing also our daughter could be removed from my full-time care since he was intent on moving out. In a very short space of time I was having to adapt my expectation of becoming a family of four, to one where I might be on my own. It was all a heavy burden almost too difficult to bear. At the same time, I still knew the Lord's hand was in this somehow and He had allowed and even purposed it all. I really had to battle self-pity and depression, and admittedly I was upset with the Lord for making me stoop so low only to be rejected. This defeat felt so unjust to me and the taunts of the enemy were palpable.

The Lord got me through this time and I strengthened myself in Him again. Out of an effort of the will I had to reframe my thinking: *I have entered this world with nothing, if I can leave with just Jesus, I have gained everything. God has the right to give and take away yet I am to keep praising. Not my will, but His will be done.* The lessons I had to learn would surpass the temporary affliction of my soul. Was this not the cost of knowing Him, to share in His sufferings?

He was like a zombie bereft of any feeling or emotion

Sometime after this, whilst we were still both in the home living our separate lives, there appeared to be a break-through. Michael requested to talk to me and there was some effort to reconcile, although no repentance was shown. He allowed me to pray for him. This 'return' to the marriage only lasted two days in which he appeared lifeless, in a daze and like there was a heavy weight or dark cloud over him. He was like a zombie bereft of any feeling or emotion. Even his pride and confidence were now submerged. The Lord directed me to show love, care and physical affection towards Michael during that time. This paved the way for him to open up to me, saying he was aware of a spiritual attack and that he felt confused, even stating he was worried he was losing his mind.

Two days later, having remained in this state, he found the pressure too much and said he couldn't love me – he'd tried – but wanted to separate still.

For he who doubts is like a wave of the sea driven and tossed by the wind. For let not that man suppose that he will receive anything from the Lord; he is a double-minded man, unstable in all his ways.

James 1:6-8

8.

Harp And Spear

Attempting to justify it with scripture

Michael moved out around March 2021 (two to three months after the announcement of his leaving) to live in a caravan on the land owned by his family. It was not long before he was talking of divorce, attempting to justify it with scripture and a sensation he referred to as the Holy Spirit giving him peace regarding the decision. I knew there were no legal or biblical grounds for Michael to divorce me yet he used threatening language to try to get me to conform to his will to make it easier for him. The Lord led me to make a stand and resist this, which I did but it was always followed by opposition.

I could not keep playing the harp to someone who wanted to throw spears at me

Michael messaged me that month asking how I would feel about him having second thoughts regarding the marriage. He claimed his heart had been changing and that God had spoken to him in his thoughts saying, *Go back to your wife.* When collecting Rebecca from the home he showed affection (albeit superficial) and reiterated this sentiment. The home had been peaceful since he had left (a new dynamic) but the possibility of his imminent return filled me with dread. I recalled and identified with the narrative of David and Saul:

> *But the Spirit of the LORD departed from Saul, and a distressing spirit from the LORD troubled him. And Saul's servants said to him, 'Surely, a distressing spirit from God is troubling you. Let our master now command your servants, who are before you, to seek out a man who is a*

skilful player on the harp. And it shall be that he will play it with his hand when the distressing spirit from God is upon you, and you shall be well.'

1 Samuel 16:14-16

Saul, who had once been close to David, became jealous of him, turning against him. I also noticed there was a spiritual jealously from Michael towards me. David would minister to Saul by playing the harp but Saul, twice, threw spears at him. David had to escape and flee. I could not keep playing the harp to someone who would continue to throw spears at me. There is a time, as there was for David, for separation and taking refuge.

I could not trust his words alone

Just as David displayed great respect towards Saul, I needed to continue to respect and submit to Michael, as someone who still held authority over me. However, I did not feel the Lord wanted Michael back in the home at this time in order for the Lord to deal with him on his own, away from Rebecca and me. By this time I had reached out to my church and they had started to pray regularly with me. I shared with them that I would need to see the fruit of repentance and a change in him before he returned. I began to see a cyclical pattern in Michael's requests to reconcile followed by a retraction of the request. I could not trust his words alone.

No one else in my life knew of what I was going through

The support from a select few people, including two pastors, during this time was a real strength. Being accountable to an authority ensured I handled the situation as wisely and maturely as possible. They counselled me through the difficulties without imposing their views. Instead, they created an environment where I could freely share and seek the Lord with them regarding His direction for each scenario I was faced with. Aside from these select few, no one else in my life knew what I was going through, including my own family. It was important to me that I had no one else's expectations placed upon me and I had the liberty and space to obey Christ as I saw Him leading me.

Sure enough, Michael's insistence and determination to return soon dwindled and he no longer pursued this. The test of time proved this desire to restore the marriage was not genuine. The Lord was keeping me close to Himself and guiding me in how to pray for Michael. I believed He revealed to me that there was a pharisaical spirit at play within his family and I started to pray against this. There was also a history of using Ouija boards, interaction with the demonic and a continuation of a number of supernatural experiences amongst his family members, some of which they had attributed to the Holy Spirit.

But whoever causes one of these little ones who believe in Me to sin, it would be better for him if a millstone were hung around his neck, and he were drowned in the depth of the sea.

Matthew 18:6

9.

A Lesson In Righteousness

Covid took a back seat in my life in comparison to everything else I was dealing with

In the midst of all that was unfolding in my marriage, I tried to keep everything as normal and as peaceful as possible for Rebecca, mindful that I was not to neglect giving her attention. Maintaining a focus on her needs and development at this crucial and impressionable age of seven years old was essential. The events of Covid, of course, contributed significantly towards our isolation, yet I was probably one of very few people that could say Covid took a back seat in my life in comparison to everything else I was dealing with.

I don't have a natural disposition for being outspoken

Following an online presentation by Rebecca's school regarding their policy on 'Relationships and Sex Education', I became grieved and saddened in my spirit at what she may be exposed to. I gave it some time and prayer but the burden did not go away. I knew I would have to write to the headteacher. I don't have a natural disposition for being outspoken, nor was I enthused at being a forerunner in these matters. I was already immersed in an intense battle, yet for the sake of righteousness I needed to make a stand.

Somehow, one morning, the grace was there to write a letter. I wrote graciously but firmly to Rebecca's headteacher about my concerns regarding the agenda to promote and disproportionately normalise same-sex partnerships, which only make up a small minority of the population. Being a Church of England school, I described how the foundational principles of the Bible were increasingly being manipulated, which grieved

God, especially when His own church endorsed and promoted these lies. I added how it took away my control as her parent to approach these issues in the way and at the age I deemed appropriate.

The enemy was quick to try putting me off sending this letter, bringing to my attention that my own home life was a mess and who was I to try and be a voice on this matter when Rebecca wasn't receiving the modelling of a biblical marriage in the house? I pushed these thoughts to one side and sent the letter, asking for prayer from my church family regarding the response it would prompt.

She had been losing sleep over this

Soon after, I received a phone call from the headteacher. She thanked me for my letter and confessed to me she had been losing sleep over this and it had been playing on her conscience. I had always believed her to be a born-again believer so was encouraged at least that this policy disturbed her. She admitted her hands felt tied but there was one other Christian couple who had approached her over the same issue. I tried to encourage her and she discussed ways with me of how they wanted to get around this. The Lord encouraged me through this – that we should never disqualify ourselves from being a voice on these matters. I was not a bold person and my life at this point looked hopeless, yet God still wanted to use me and imparted His words, His grace and His boldness to enable me to speak out, irrespective of my circumstances.

Be merciful to me, O God, be merciful to me! For my soul trusts in You; and in the shadow of Your wings I will make my refuge, until these calamities have passed by.

Psalm 57:1

10.

Until These Calamities Have Passed By

My status had been demoted from a wife to that of a concubine

What proceeded to unravel over the months that followed Michael's departure were intense battles and a real 'yo-yoing' of his behaviour and emotions. He would come to the home when he liked to see Rebecca and I felt the Lord would have me show him hospitality, including inviting him to join us for meals and giving him money when he asked. It was as if my status had been demoted from a wife to that of a concubine. Whilst degrading, I did all things unto Christ by His grace and through His strength. However, there were also times I believed the Lord permitted me to stand against certain requests, receiving His full protection in doing so. At best this period of time was civil and calm, but at its worst, the following episodes occurred:

- Michael became suicidal, on at least one occasion disclosing in a message to me he had gone as far as positioning a rope.

- Threatening divorce, then restraining from going ahead with it, only to pursue it again (I lost count of the amount of times this happened).

- He continued to pursue a relationship with the Irish woman on Facebook and planned to move there. He told our daughter of these plans. After waging warfare in prayer, he relented on this. Just days later, the move was on again, so it was back to prayer with those who were supporting me. He then cancelled the visit. On a separate occasion she had planned to visit him but, through prayer, this was resisted (Michael had become annoyed and fed up with her over something and stopped her coming).

Due to this course of events he'd sensed I'd been praying, asking me, *'Have you prayed against this?'* I responded, *'Of course.'* He'd known there had been an external force at work in how it had all played out.

- He had an episode of heavy drinking.
- One evening Michael punched a man in the town who was very drunk and apparently posing a threat. He fell unconscious and an ambulance was called. Michael fled the scene and was immediately broken, remorseful and fearful of police involvement. As he often did when he was in trouble and broken, he came to see me for prayer and claimed he would come back to church. Although the police were called to investigate this incident, he was not identified as the culprit. Michael then fell unwell and couldn't attend church. Subsequently, this desire to come to church subsided. It seemed his 'repentance' once again had not been genuine.

Where he was faithless, I needed to remain faithful

Despite Michael's abuse and betrayal towards me, the Lord gave me much love and forgiveness towards Michael, which I myself could not have naturally possessed. Where sin abounded, God's grace abounded so much more. I believed I needed to keep ministering to Michael (whilst separate from him) and remain faithful to him and to my marriage vows. Where he was faithless, I needed to remain faithful, just as God is towards me. In this, God showed me the extent of His mercy and love towards a rebellious sinner. The faith was given by the Lord to keep interceding for his soul and to fight to preserve the marriage. As I read through the book of Hosea in the Bible, God imparted to me something of His hurt and pain over the rejection of those He has so faithfully loved, depicting also the current state of Israel and the church. It was precious to be trusted to bear and share in something of God's pain and burden, and the following song was birthed.

****

I loved you, from the beginning,
I loved you
And I called you, out of bondage
I called you

I led you, with cords of love,
I led you
And I fed you, stooped low,
I fed you

You forgot me, looked away
And forgot me
You chose another, for your bread
Chose another

You set your heart, on iniquity
You set your heart
And you worshipped, to someone else
Gave your worship.

I'll let the wind wrap you up in its wings,
Set you in a dry plain
Turn your glory into shame
So you thirst for me again

Then I will come like the rain to heal and bind,
Once I've stricken and torn
And you're lost and forlorn
So My mercy you will mourn

I'll be faithful, to the faithless
I'll be faithful
I'll show mercy, over justice,
I'll show mercy

And I'll receive you, if you humbly return
I'll receive you
I will restore, My beloved
I will restore.

For I am
God, not,
Man
The holy One in your midst

****

LYRICS FROM 'HOSEA'
2020 SONG BY HANNAH

Stand fast therefore in the liberty by which Christ has made us free, and do not be entangled again with a yoke of bondage.

Galatians 5:1

11.

Captive Set Free?

Soon enough I was being accused of having an affair

Following the discovery of a wedding picture found randomly in a board game during a gathering at my home in December 2021, Lydia suggested that I put the picture above the fireplace on display. It would stand as a visual sign, before the enemy, of the contending for my husband and marriage.

The following month, Michael accused me of acting inappropriately with another male solely because the male was single and had been fellowshipping in my Christian circle. He had also been one of my WhatsApp contacts. I had never been alone with this man nor had there been any inappropriate correspondence. However, he believed my Christian friends were purposely inviting him and were encouraging everything he speculated. Soon enough I was being accused of having an affair, which was completely unfounded! For three days I received abusive texts containing religious, slanderous and filthy language. The messages came one after the other and included praying curses over me. It was so relentless that I knew the breaks in the messages occurred when he was sleeping. Such energy to persist in this was undoubtedly demonic in nature.

There were concerns for the safety of Rebecca and me

Michael started posting messages on Lydia's and my worship music channels on YouTube, and there were serious threats for the male in question. He was determined to come to a church meeting with some family members to publicly rebuke me. I had to block him on my phone. Around this time, I came home once and found the wedding picture torn to pieces and left for me to see. As I put up other wedding pictures the same thing would happen to them all. There were concerns for the safety of Rebecca and me, with alternative accommodation being offered to us, but I decided I could not go anywhere indefinitely and would need to face Michael at some point. I declined and trusted the Lord would protect us and restrain him.

Because I had blocked him, he eventually came to the home unexpectedly. I remember the momentary anxiety I would experience each time I heard the sound of him entering through the front door. On this occasion I was particularly fearful. This fear must have shown on my face because the first thing he said was that he wasn't going to hurt me and he needed prayer as he had been so angry he could have killed someone. I told him he needed deliverance, to which he admitted he probably did. I explained I'd want elders to administer any such ministry but he wanted me to do it then and there, stating I had the authority of the Holy Spirit. So, succumbing to the fact there was truth in that, rather out of my depth, I asked the Holy Spirit to help me.

Michael felt an immediate lightness

I believe the Holy Spirit had us declare forgiveness towards each other to start with. As Michael had felt wronged, it seemed he still needed to forgive me, even though I was innocent of his accusations. For three hours things were brought into the light. Michael openly admitted what he was struggling with and taking each particular struggle we then prayed into them. There were signs of humility and repentance and some demonic entities were identified. As a teenager, he'd foolishly prayed for a spirit that had given him some supernatural ability and skill in fighting. We also specifically asked the Lord to name the demon that had appeared before a friend one night when she'd prayed for Michael. Out of his mouth came its name.

After praying against some things, Michael felt an immediate lightness. It was the first time in a long while he had openly admitted the various issues and battles he was facing. He said he was committed to coming to church and left the house calm, with a notable rest and peace upon him that evening. I was drained and exhausted but hopeful as I'd known the Holy Spirit leading me in this. The only thing I was aware of that Michael had not properly acknowledged was the religious spirit and spiritual abuse perpetrated towards me. There had been no repentance in this area.

When an unclean spirit goes out of a man, he goes through dry places, seeking rest, and finds none. Then he says, 'I will return to my house from which I came.' And when he comes, he finds it empty, swept, and put in order. Then he goes and takes with him seven other spirits more wicked than himself, and they enter and dwell there; and the last state of that man is worse than the first. So shall it also be with this wicked generation.

Matthew 12:43-45

12.

An Angry Man Stirs Up Strife

I needed to stand fast in liberty

Michael was quiet the next day, then he messaged saying the enemy was starting to get into his head again and so I told him to resist the devil. Unfortunately, he slipped back into his unsettled patterns once more and wanted to impose a rule that meant I would not join in any fellowship or gathering where single men were present. I could not pre-empt who would be present at certain meetings and therefore could not submit to this. Living under such rules and conditions would be burdensome. I knew even if I had agreed to try and keep to his requests, the enemy would then attempt implementing additional rules, continuing to demand more ground. The nature of obtaining power and control over someone usually involves 'goal posts' continually changing. I was not going to come into any agreement with this enemy ploy and knew I needed to stand fast in liberty. However, my refusal to submit to this demand left me susceptible to suffer the consequences of his displeasure.

If I'd been a man he'd have punched me in the face

Soon after, Michael messaged to say he had started the divorce process online. There were incidents at the home where he would take my mobile and delete all the conversations I'd been having with the two pastors I was in touch with regarding him. Enraged at my continuation of fellowship groups which included the single man he'd accused, Michael took our whole wedding album and said he would be burning it. He said to me if I'd been a man he'd have punched me in the face. Although she hadn't been allowed to say, Rebecca told me he'd disclosed to her how he'd parked away from the house one night. He'd then walked up to my car to check if my brake pads had been warm to ascertain if we'd been out. There was also another incident where he had been messaging me whilst he was watching outside the home.

And they said to him, 'We each have had a dream, and there is no interpreter of it.' So Joseph said to them, 'Do not interpretations belong to God?'

Genesis 40:8

13.

Prophetic Dreams

Squeezing tighter and tighter to suffocate me to death

Amidst the trials I began to have dreams, which I believe were from the Lord. In one dream, a very large snake bit me and began coiling itself around me, squeezing tighter and tighter to suffocate me to death. After what felt like a very long wrestle, somehow the snake died. At the end of the dream I saw its dead face with a damaged eye. This made me think of the religious spirit as represented by a snake – John the Baptist referred to the Pharisees as a 'brood of vipers' (see Matthew 12:34). Luke 10:19 also states we have been given authority to trample upon snakes, to overcome the power of the enemy and that nothing will harm us. Acts 28:3-6 details how Paul's poisonous snake bite had no effect on him. He was completely unharmed, as I had been in the dream.

He was not escaping to his freedom

I also had another vivid dream one night. I was in my bedroom with Rebecca and we became aware of a butterfly in the room. It was disruptive, flapping about and wouldn't settle. We opened the window to let it out but for some reason it would not fly out. It consumed our attention, sometimes even flying into us, causing us to step backwards. I then knew I had to wait for it to settle against the window and pull across the curtain to restrict the space in which it had to move, in the hope it would be forced to fly out of the open window. I woke up after the curtain was pulled across, not knowing if the butterfly had managed to escape. I knew Michael was represented by this butterfly (he would have hated a portrayal of himself as such a delicate creature!) but like this butterfly he was fearful, chaotic and unsettled, causing distress to Rebecca and me. We'd tried to help him but he was not escaping to his freedom, even though we had shown him the way (the open window). The curtain in the dream represented a divide or separation needed from him. It portrayed a need to be out of sight, restricting the movement and freedom he had in our lives, in order that it may actually help him and preserve us.

Soon after this dream I was shown the following verses:

When he had taken him and brought him to his mother, he sat on her knees till noon, and then died. And she went up and laid him on the bed of the man of God, shut the door upon him, and went out.

2 Kings 4:20-21

The Shunammite woman (the mother in these verses) came to the realisation that she had to shut the door upon her dead son and go to seek the man of God. It was now time to commit Michael to God and separate myself from him instead of continuing to bear the weight myself.

God sets the solitary in families; He brings out those
who are bound into prosperity;
but the rebellious dwell in a dry land.

Psalm 68:6

14.

God Sets The Solitary In Families

I sought the Lord asking if I would also be moving to this area

Running parallel to the frequent dramas, which had been in my life for many months now, was the support and fellowship of a prayer group that had been a great strength to me. We had been seeking God's will regarding a work He was initiating in the southern region of Hampshire. It was becoming apparent the Lord was calling individuals to move to the Havant area, forty minutes' drive from my current residence. I sought the Lord asking if I would also be moving to this area or if I had to continue a further time of solitude where I was. It transpired that I was tied into a fixed term in my rented accommodation until November 2022 (eleven months away), so I glumly concluded that the Lord's answer must be to stay put.

However, one prayer evening, the group felt burdened to ask the Lord. Amazingly, the very next day, having reported some issues in the property to the landlord's manager, I was told that because the works were extensive, I could be released from the tenancy.

*Thus says the L*ORD *God of Israel: 'Let My people go,*
that they may hold a feast to Me in the wilderness.'
*And Pharaoh said, 'Who is the L*ORD*,*
that I should obey His voice to let Israel go?
*I do not know the L*ORD*, nor will I let Israel go.'*

Exodus 5:1-2

15.

Let My People Go

I had a very uneasy feeling and trepidation in my spirit

By this time, Michael had been living away from the home for almost a year, although he still came to the property to see Rebecca, do his washing and have baths, etc. I tentatively told him in a message that the property needed work and I believed the Lord was calling Rebecca and me to live in the Havant area. Havant was actually the same distance for him to see Rebecca from where he currently lived, just in the opposite direction. It was closer to his parents' home. Initially it looked like he had partially accepted the idea of us moving but then the resistance commenced.

I received a message from Michael one day saying that he was coming over as God had put something on his heart, after keeping him awake all night. He was determined that I would listen. I really wanted to be left alone and tried to deter him from coming but he told me not to dictate to him and reiterated that he **would** be coming and that I would be listening and was not to be disobedient. I had a very uneasy feeling and trepidation in my spirit. He would not tell me his time of arrival, only that he'd come *'when the Lord leads'*. There was no one I could ask to be with me as I was quite isolated where I lived in the countryside. I messaged a friend and a pastor who knew of the situation. They committed to praying for me and, having seen the messages, the pastor confirmed Michael was not speaking to me as someone who was influenced by the Holy Spirit.

I would need a face like flint

I had become accustomed to hiding my phone the minute I heard Michael's car pull up, because he would go through my messages or delete them. I kept a work mobile phone accessible in case I needed to call someone. I knew he would forcefully try and dissuade me from moving and that I would need a face like flint. This would be a time to stand. When he showed up, he disclosed that the Lord had told him to reconcile with me and move back in. I told him this was not what the Lord had shown me and that I was moving (all the while remembering the butterfly dream and scripture confirming separation was needed). I told him I didn't want to talk with him and I had nothing further to say. He wanted me to pray about it with him but the spirit he came in was not the Holy Spirit. I had no peace or freedom to pray with him. In response to my refusal to pray, he told me I was disobedient and spiteful towards him.

He got to the doors and took my keys

I wanted to leave the house but he got to the doors and took my keys so I couldn't leave. Where I was not obeying his words, he resorted to physically intervening to prevent me trying to leave his presence. He stated he was moving back in whether I wanted it or not. He was deceived and confused – my battle was not against flesh and blood. There was an unspoken ultimatum at play here – Michael was offering a new start with him if I didn't move to the area he considered a dump and full of riff-raff. I knew the 'dump' and 'riff-raff' was the exact place and people the Lord was calling me to and the enemy was attempting to prevent a move.

Being trapped in the house (and having nowhere to go should I even get out), I announced I was going to take a bath and retrieved my phone. With the door safely locked, I think I took the longest bath I've ever had, and sent messages to those who had been praying. They held an urgent prayer meeting for me that night praying for 'Pharaoh' to let me go.

I was back to having space again

Michael ended up moving back out after a couple of nights and I was back to having space again, although he still had his key to the house, meaning that I could never fully be at peace there. Before his departure, he'd spoken to the landlord's manager and told him 'we' were not moving out anymore and that in his opinion the work needed on the house was not as essential as it had first appeared.

The time had come for me to disclose to the landlord's manager and Rebecca's headteacher the difficulties we were facing at home and that Michael had not been resident there for a year. I told them I needed to move and received sympathetic and supportive responses.

****

Heavy darkness looms, set to increase
Keep me, O Lord, in Your perfect peace
Stationed on the Rock, eyes to behold
Coming wonders, that by faith unfold

Would I, when heat comes, each side hard pressed,
Ooze Your perfume, that You may be blessed,
Through each hidden scar, please conform me
To Your likeness, firmly planted tree

Keep me clinging to Your promises
As You keep holding me in Your truths
A vessel for honour, have Your way in me,
That the world might see Your glory

This narrowing path, claims more of me
Help me, O Lord, unyoke willingly,
Cleaving to life's source, the one true vine
Pow'r from on high, to arise and shine

Stranger journeying, sorrows to bear
Comfort me, Lord, until I get there
Walk uncompromised, steps to be just
Stewarding all that You, Lord, entrust

You will never leave me, nor forsake me,
Nothing can separate me from Your love.
You will never leave me, nor forsake me,
Nothing can separate.

****

LYRICS FROM 'KEEP ME'
2021 SONG BY HANNAH

This Book of the Law shall not depart from your mouth, but you shall meditate in it day and night, that you may observe to do according to all that is written in it. For then you will make your way prosperous, and then you will have good success. Have I not commanded you? Be strong and of good courage; do not be afraid, nor be dismayed, for the LORD your God is with you wherever you go.

Joshua 1:8-9

16.

The Cat Conundrum

Our cat was starting to look suspiciously larger

I started searching for private rental properties in the Havant and Emsworth area. Many I enquired about either were already taken or didn't take pets. To complicate matters, our cat was starting to look suspiciously larger and I was convinced she was pregnant. Cats only have a pregnancy span of two months and she was probably already a month along. Either I had to move before the kittens came or I was needing a landlord to accept a single mother with about seven cats (not the most attractive profile).

I was not fussy and I needed to get away

However, a property situated in-between Havant and Emsworth became available and viewings for all those interested were scheduled for the same day, so I booked to view. It was a three-bedroom property (I only needed two bedrooms) and there was not much to like or dislike. I was not fussy and I needed to get away so I prayed to the Lord and believed I should show my interest. I was told there were about nine other viewings of the property. Those wanting the property had to just put in their offers and the landlord would choose. Knowing there was much competition, I offered to pay six months rent up front and said I would move as soon as possible. Miraculously, I was offered the property and a move-in date was set for around two weeks later!

You will keep him in perfect peace, whose mind is stayed on You, because he trusts in You. Trust in the L<small>ORD</small> forever, for in Y<small>AH</small>, the L<small>ORD</small>, is everlasting strength.

Isaiah 26:3-4

17.

A Storm Is Brewing

I tentatively and discreetly tried to pack

Knowing how much Michael was opposed to me moving and, due to the unpredictability of his actions, I thought it best not to tell him we'd found a property. Instead, the plan was to move out without him knowing. However, I knew that I would need to tell Rebecca. It posed a bit of a dilemma for me, expecting a child to keep from her father that we had found somewhere to move to, but the story of Rahab and her cover-up of the truth proved helpful for this discussion. Rebecca, in her wisdom, agreed not telling him was the right way to approach it.

I tentatively and discreetly tried to pack various items knowing he was still turning up at the property from time to time. It proved an impossible task as I could not pack anything Michael might notice was missing when he came around. Additionally, I couldn't have packing boxes on view.

I hit brick walls

The next sticking point came when disclosing to my landlord's agents that I was moving. As Michael was a joint tenant and we were within a fixed term, I was not able to hand in notice on behalf of both of us. It would require a 'deed of surrender' to be signed by myself and Michael (and the landlord) to release us from the tenancy, otherwise there was the legal obligation to cover rent up until the end of the fixed term (up until November). I could not afford rent on two properties. If I didn't get Michael to sign the agreement, we could not be released. Knowing the housing law myself, I looked for ways around this and even into clauses and loop holes relating to domestic abuse victims but I hit brick walls. There was nothing. It was a hurdle I had overlooked. I had no choice but to tell Michael we had found somewhere.

The accusations against me began again

I carefully phrased to Michael that he would be responsible for paying the rent when we left if he didn't sign the agreement. This seemed to work as he wasn't at that point contributing anything financially to us. He did not believe it was the Lord's will that Rebecca and I move as he had not given his consent for it. The accusations against me began again – that I was deceived and was not submissive to his authority. But at least he was prepared to sign the agreement. There was always a paradox present with Michael: he wanted divorce yet to retain authority over me; he wanted to live apart yet control where we lived; he had pursued another relationship yet condemned one he incorrectly accused me of having.

For the Lord GOD will help Me; therefore I will not be disgraced; therefore I have set My face like a flint, and I know that I will not be ashamed. He is near who justifies Me; who will contend with Me? Let us stand together. Who is My adversary? Let him come near Me.

Isaiah 50:7-8

18.

Get Moving

I put my hands over Rebecca's ears so she wouldn't hear

That same evening, Michael was due to collect Rebecca from the house. There had been a power cut. My mobile network was down, there was no heating and it was starting to get dark and cold. When he arrived he immediately demanded that none of the furniture be removed from the property. He demanded 50 per cent of it all and said not to touch it because he'd be back over in a couple of days to photograph it. I explained to him that I had bought most of it and some of it had been given or loaned to us by my family. He had no use for such furniture in a caravan whereas Rebecca and I needed it. All we had jointly purchased was the sofa.

He became verbally abusive to me in front of Rebecca – cursing and praying judgement over me. I put my hands over Rebecca's ears so she wouldn't hear and prayed over his words in tongues, blessing and forgiving him. This frustrated him. At one point he said to Rebecca she wouldn't be seeing him again and she promptly burst into tears. I told her she was to stay with me that night but then he apologised to her and asked if she'd go with him. I didn't want her going with him in his current state but I knew to protest would escalate his behaviour. With Rebecca witnessing all of this, it was not wise to provoke him further. To keep the environment calm, I asked if she was sure she was okay to go with him and she nodded. He then took her.

I was left in a dark, cold house with no means of communication and I wanted Rebecca with me. I thought to check my work mobile and this was working so I messaged Lydia all that had happened. She told me to pack a bag and stay with them that night, which I did.

We hurriedly packed up boxes

The next day Lydia and her husband, Stefan, helped to remove the furniture and take it to my parents' house. We all drove the forty-minute journey from their home in Havant back home and started dismantling the furniture. I had informed my parents that Michael wanted to sell the furniture, a lot of which they'd paid for or given as a present, so they also helped load cars to get as much as we could out of the house. It was surprising how much furniture – even a double mattress! – we could squeeze into cars.

We hurriedly packed up boxes of other possessions in no particular order. It was far from the organised way I would usually address a house move but there was a sense of speed needed – after all, this was no normal house move.

He decided not to return Rebecca to my care that day

As the afternoon progressed, Stefan had an increased sense of urgency in his spirit, believing we needed to leave the property quickly since we didn't know when Michael would be bringing Rebecca back. I'd messaged Michael asking him to drop her at my parents' house but he wouldn't comply. We exited the house quickly and I drove to my mum and dad's, where I would have to sleep due to no longer having a bed at home. There was now limited furniture there but our pregnant cat would have to stay put for now.

No sooner had I driven to my parents' house ten minutes away than Michael messaged. He'd just been to our home. We would have missed him by just a few minutes and my friends would have undoubtedly driven past him without knowing. As an act of retaliation for removal of the furniture, he decided not to return Rebecca to my care that day.

He stated I had mentally abused him throughout the marriage

Prior to this event, Michael had decided to halt the divorce process but now he was pursuing it again. I'd received papers which revealed that he had cited his grounds for divorce as 'unreasonable behaviour'. Other grounds available to him were: adultery, desertion, separation for two years (where both parties agree to the divorce) or five years separation.[3] He stated I had mentally abused him throughout the marriage disregarding his opinions.

I had three options. I could ignore this and not file an 'answer'. This would default my position to one accepting the petitioner's (the petitioner being Michael) claim and grounds. The next option was to 'cross petition'. This meant I would be agreeing to divorce but not on the grounds presented by the petitioner, allowing me to present my own grounds for divorce. Finally, I could 'defend'/'contend' the divorce. This meant to disagree with and object to getting divorced on the basis it did not meet any of the legal grounds. I believed the Lord wanted me to 'defend'. Michael had no legal or biblical grounds – was I not to fight for him and our marriage?

---

3   See page 194 for statistics on divorce.

After whom has the king of Israel come out? Whom do you pursue? A dead dog? A flea? Therefore let the Lᴏʀᴅ be judge, and judge between you and me, and see and plead my case, and deliver me out of your hand.

1 Samuel 24:14-15

19.

Let The Lord Judge Between Me And You

Once I'd taken this step there would be no going back

The next day I discovered that Michael had called the police to the property to report me for removing the items of furniture. I knew now that I too had to approach the police to disclose all that had been going on as he still had our daughter and had not returned her. I did not want her to be used as a weapon of control over me. I was so nervous contacting the police as I had never disclosed his behaviour to authorities before and it felt like I was being disloyal to my husband. It felt like once I'd taken this step there would be no going back. However, at the same time, I knew he had gone too far and it was now a matter of safety for Rebecca and me. I needed her back and we needed protection for the two-week interim period until we could get into our new home.

They would want to arrest him

I was interviewed by the police and answered their questions honestly. I'd provided a record of all the incidents, the dates when they occurred and evidence from text messages. The police were thorough and questioned me on historic incidents too. I told them I did not need him arrested and it wasn't about punishment. I merely needed something like an order (I knew from the nature of work that I did that they could issue a DVPO – domestic violence protection order) to give short-term protection and breathing space. I was told that based on what I'd said, they would want to arrest him. I asked what the possible charges could be and was informed it could be any of the following: threats to kill, coercive control, harassment, stalking, false imprisonment and ABH (actual bodily harm).

He answered *'no comment'* to every question

It was a number of days before the police got hold of Michael, leaving me with no bail conditions to prevent him contacting me. I couldn't get an emergency injunction whilst this action was still outstanding as you cannot have both a bail condition and injunction in place at the same time. Michael eventually attended the police station for an interview. His solicitor had prepared a statement and he answered *'no comment'* to every question. I was featured on the MARAC (multi-agency risk assessment conference) agenda, which is a regular regional meeting held by the police to enable various professionals to come together and discuss the safeguarding of specific high-risk domestic abuse cases. I'd been disappointed with the handling of my case by the police due to their main emphasis being on Michael's arrest rather than our immediate protection. All I'd needed was relief from contact from him for two weeks to allow us to move, but his communication continued, albeit cautious in nature.

He did, however, turn up at church

Michael began to express that he wanted to be reconciled to me, showing me screen shots proving he'd emailed the court to cancel the divorce process. I responded by saying that I would need to see fruit to his repentance over time. I said he would need to start by meeting my pastor alone, reiterating that his previous actions could still have consequences. This was not the quick solution he was hoping for, especially as police processes would still go ahead and I was still going to move house in accordance to God's calling. Thus, he never pursued this help from our pastor.

He did, however, turn up at church, but rather than it be for the sake of his soul, it was to convince the pastor as to why he was within his rights to divorce me based on his interpretation of a certain scripture. My pastor disagreed with Michael's stance on this matter but handled the conversation discerningly and sensitively. He kept the door open for Michael to approach him for help and support should he desire.

This outcome sent the message to victims that they were not believed

Many weeks later I was informed by the police that the case against Michael would not be going to the CPS (Crown Prosecution Service) due to lack of evidence. I had been expecting this outcome. However, I was now able to fully understand why victims of domestic abuse do not go to the police.[4] The process had been long, arduous and emotionally taxing and this outcome sent the message to victims that they were not believed.

---

4   See page 192 for statistics on domestic abuse.

When the whirlwind passes by, the wicked is no more,
but the righteous has an everlasting foundation.

Proverbs 10:25

20.

Eye Of The Storm

I was effectively homeless, living out of a bag

The week leading up to the physical move was one of the most hard-pressed and intense periods of my life. Rebecca and I were effectively homeless, living out of a bag at my parents' home and dealing with three legal processes: the police process, the deed of surrender for leaving the property, and defending against the divorce. I was trying to clear out and clean the property whilst feeding our cat there twice a day (all the while avoiding Michael who seemed to still be turning up there but still hadn't signed the 'deed of surrender' document I'd left out for him). The 'deed of surrender' document would hold me liable for paying rent for a further month from the date it was signed, so each day that it remained unsigned, the greater the cost it was incurring for me.

I had a number of professionals I needed to liaise with including police, social services, outreach services and the agents for the new property, with their legal paperwork to complete. I was also applying for schools for Rebecca and, to top it off, I'd been covering my manager's role whilst she'd been on a sabbatical and we were experiencing issues with staff shortages alongside some intense cases to deal with.

Drawing us out of many waters

It was such a physically and emotionally demanding time with multiple pressures like I'd never known before. I disclosed very little to my parents regarding the issues with Michael in order to guard their hearts, but having them cover the simple task of cooking for Rebecca and me was a real relief and blessing as it was one less thing to do.

Two out of the three schools applied for were fully subscribed but the closest one, just a ten-minute walk away from our new house, had space for Rebecca. We moved house on Friday 4th March 2022, collecting her new school uniform on this day ready to start school on the Monday. God had safely got us to our place of refuge in record time, going ahead of us so that every detail fell into place. It was a real testimony of God's provision and deliverance, drawing us out of many waters.

Having been the last in the fellowship group to become aware I was moving, I was the first to move. Three house moves to the area soon followed and there was now a core group of about five to six households fellowshipping from the pastor's bungalow.

Watch for the storms of God. The only way God plants His saints is through the whirlwind of His storms. Will you be proven to be an empty pod with no seed inside? That will depend on whether or not you are actually living in the light of the vision you have seen. Let God send you out through His storm, and don't go until He does. If you select your own spot to be planted, you will prove yourself to be an unproductive, empty pod. However, if you allow God to plant you, you will 'bear much fruit' (John 15:8). It is essential that we live and 'walk in the light' of God's vision for us (1 John 1:7).

Oswald Chambers, *My Utmost for His Highest*

You number my wanderings; put my tears into Your bottle; are they not in Your book? When I cry out to You, then my enemies will turn back; this I know, because God is for me.

Psalm 56:8-9

21.

For Behold, The Winter Is Past

The scent of new life brought with it a fresh hope that had been long awaited

Spring was emerging, an array of daffodils had sprung up along the front path to our new abode, and just a few days before Rebecca's eighth birthday our cat gave birth to four beautiful and healthy kittens. The scent of new life brought with it a fresh hope that had been long awaited. Knowing very little about the area we had moved to, Rebecca and I spent the first few weeks and months exploring our new surroundings.

We continued to pray for Michael each night as we had been doing over the past year. We still had faith the Lord would deal with him and he would one day be restored, firstly to the Lord and then to his family. God had cultivated in me a swiftness to forgive and I would not slander him, especially to Rebecca who adored her father. He had not rejected her, only me, and I encouraged their relationship. I never allowed him to come to our new home and would take Rebecca to where he was, or to his parents' home for them to have time together.

I had been acquainted with much sorrow which I learned to bear and carry

The Lord had miraculously preserved Rebecca despite all she had endured and witnessed. She was peaceful and joyful – a delight and blessing to me, adapting so well to many changes and challenges. A teacher during a parents' evening even praised her for being a calming influence for the other children, commenting that she was emotionally mature and rarely fazed.

God had kept my heart soft towards Michael throughout the tribulations but of course healing was needed following the rejection, abuse, betrayal and trauma of all that was endured. Knowing I was in God's will offered me safety, protection and peace of mind. The new environment and location by the sea lent itself well to this healing process and I took time going on walks with the Lord, allowing His Spirit to gently minister to me. I had been acquainted with much sorrow, which I learned to bear and carry.

I was beginning to understand the blessing of suffering

A beautiful mystery began to emerge; alongside the sorrow, joy existed, of which the Lord gave me plenty. He poured upon me such love and acceptance and I felt blessed. I was beginning to understand the blessing of suffering and see it as God's grace that enabled a closeness and fellowship with Him I couldn't have otherwise known. My heart was filled with thankfulness for His goodness towards me.

****

You have worked out such love from
A spirit bruised and pained
Joy in abundance born from
Sorrow You ordained

You have kept count of my tossings
Put my tears in Your bottle
Tenderly, You have looked on me

How blessed am I?
How loved am I?
Suffering is Your grace
The door into this place
Here You unveil more
Give the sweetest glimpse
Of my Saviour's face

You freed unto great heights from
The snare set by the proud
Worked in a steadfast heart from
Affliction You allowed

You cover me with Your feathers
Under Your wings I take refuge
Tenderly, You sing over me

****

Lyrics from 'How Blessed Am I?'
2022 Song by Hannah

But if the unbeliever departs, let him depart;
a brother or a sister is not under bondage in such cases.
But God has called us to peace.

1 Corinthians 7:15

22.

But God Has Called Us To Peace?

We cannot just simply walk away when things get tough

One prayer meeting, we were joined by a visiting evangelist known to our fellowship. The group had prayed into my situation with Michael and for his soul as we often faithfully did, but afterwards the evangelist shared with me the following verse: *'But if the unbeliever departs, let him depart; a brother or a sister is not under bondage in such cases. But God has called us to peace'* (1 Corinthians 7:15).

Frankly, I was a little offended that this single man presumed it was okay to share a verse when he had no clue what I had been through and the faith God had given me to righteously stand in defending marriage in this day, when divorce was rife in our society. He had no idea what it was to remain faithful to an unfaithful spouse and that we cannot just simply throw in the towel when things get tough, picking and choosing scriptures that suited our feelings. It was about obedience to what God had called me to do. I knew he meant well but believed his good intentions were misplaced. I therefore exercised self-control and politely thanked him for sharing the verse without embracing it.

Though the fig tree may not blossom, nor fruit be on the vines; though the labour of the olive may fail, and the fields yield no food; though the flock may be cut off from the fold, and there be no herd in the stalls – yet I will rejoice in the LORD, I will joy in the God of my salvation. The LORD God is my strength; He will make my feet like deer's feet, and He will make me walk on my high hills.

Habakkuk 3:17-19

23.

When The Enemy Comes In Like A Flood

I began to believe this was a vexing from the enemy

Many issues started to surface in the new home. I was without electricity for over twenty-four hours and needed to sleep and work elsewhere for a night and day. On two separate occasions I came home to water leaks causing flooding in the home. Although stressful, I naturally just got on and dealt with them, contacting the necessary people to fix and sort these issues.

However, as the problems persisted I began to record them, realising there were more than ten quite serious issues that had occurred in a short space of time. I began to believe this was a vexing from the enemy. We prayed about it in our prayer group and I contacted a friend who spoke to me about cleansing the property. I was a little sceptical, but willing to give it a go by this point. She talked me through what to do and after this there was a significant settling of problems within the home.

I wanted the opportunity to honour my marriage vows

Despite the screen shots sent by Michael showing a retraction of his divorce petition, it turned out he'd not followed through with this. At the last minute I was informed that the decree nisi (first stage of divorce) was due to be declared in a court miles away, in Birmingham. Having believed divorce was no longer being pursued by Michael, I had not submitted a defence against it. Now in this predicament, I sought to find out what I could do. I was told I did not need to attend court as it would not stop the process. Instead, I was advised of the form I needed to complete to submit a late defence case, which of course came with a further fee.

I continued to struggle my way through the legal processes entailed in contending the divorce, diligently seeking to educate myself on the law. Hanging over me was the glum reality that less than 1 per cent of people contend divorce and the success rate of such cases was very low. Nevertheless, I gleaned what I could from others who had wisdom on this matter. I submitted a winsome case for defending the marriage on the grounds that Michael's divorce petition did not meet the legal requirements for divorce according to the law at the time. 'No fault divorce' came into law in April 2022, during my time of 'defending', but having applied before this date, Michael's application was subject to the preceding law. I also stated he was mentally unstable and divorce was not the solution to him getting better; rather, he needed support and help. I wanted the opportunity to honour my marriage vows made before God and man, and allow time to be given for the restoration of the marriage. I would fight in faith for my family to be reunited once the Lord had dealt with him.

I worshipped the Lord and chose to accept this fate

This process took me on a path of endless hurdles and struggles. Eventually I heard back from a judge who had decided against my defence and had granted the decree nisi, ordering I pay any court costs. I was deflated and completely discouraged, questioning the Lord as to why He kept getting me to pursue courses of action which neither went in my favour or produced any fruit. His response was Habakkuk 3:17-19 (as quoted at the beginning of the chapter) telling me it was not the season for blossom on trees or fruit on the vines. I was still to rejoice because He was doing a deeper work in me; making my feet like deer's, to climb up higher. He was growing deeper roots under the ground that no one could see but it was essential foundational work for growing me into His likeness. This was more about a lasting work in me than a momentary victory. As hard as it was, and without understanding this defeat, out of obedience I worshipped the Lord and chose to accept this fate.

Michael was demanding £30,000

Apart from a few difficult messages, and an episode where Michael strongly opposed Rebecca and me flying to visit my brother in Germany, he remained mostly quiet on matters. I was really able to experience the home as a place of refuge. At least that was the case until one morning in November 2022, I received a letter from his solicitor. Michael was demanding £30,000 (as a financial settlement from the divorce) for a property I owned and was renting out. The income received from this was contributing towards the rent of the home in which Rebecca and I were currently living. About five years prior, we had received equity when selling one home and moving to another. Michael had wanted to split the equity and spent all his 50 per cent relatively quickly. Part of this money had also been made up of a substantial deposit contributed by my parents. I chose to invest my 50 per cent in a property solely in my name (as Michael showed no interest in this venture) and rented this out with a buy-to-let interest-only mortgage. It was this property he was now pursuing a share in. With mortgage rates being low at this time, I made a very good return on this investment. The profit earned through the rental income was used to provide a roof over our heads while we resided together. Michael had benefited from this.

I needed a solicitor but I knew I could not afford one

More recently it seemed the Lord had allowed my finances to diminish, yet I was able to get by, albeit without any savings. I learnt a greater dependency on the Lord in the area of finances. It now seemed Michael was after money that I didn't have, or would want to force a sale on the property taking away vital provision from Rebecca and me. It was through necessity, not choice, I had been the main breadwinner for years, providing for Michael. His course of action was both shocking and completely unjust. I also recalled times during the beginning of the separation period I had freely given him money. It was felt by my prayer group that I needed a solicitor but I knew I could not afford one. However, someone graciously offered financial assistance and so the search began for a solicitor to help defend against this new scheme of the enemy.

****

Trust and obey
When what you had yesterday
Is taken away
Trust and obey.

Always pray
For that word given yesterday
To come your way
Always pray.

Though the tree looks bear and yields no fruit
He's working underground
Growing deeper roots

Sing praise
To the One who never changes
His promises
Are yes and amen
Sing praise
To the One who never changes
By faith stand on His word again
By faith stand on His word again

Cry out to Him
When nothing but desperation
Lies within
Cry out to Him

In His time He has made all things beautiful

****

Lyrics from 'Deeper Roots'
2022 Song by Hannah

*The **LORD** will fight for you,*
and you shall hold your peace.

Exodus 14:14

24.

Saint Helen

I put all my eggs into one basket

I was signposted to the Christian Lawyers Association and my referral prompted some responses from solicitors wanting to take on my case. This would require discernment. I received a number of calls and emails. With each one, there was always something that discouraged me, either about the soliciting firm or the conversation. No faith was shown for defending the marriage by most and some actively discouraged it due to the low success rate. I felt they were just after my business and so, one by one, I eliminated solicitors, not feeling a peace to go with any of them. It left just one email, from Helen. Her email to me showed compassion for my situation and so, having turned down all the others, I put all my eggs into one basket. We arranged for her to call me at 11am that Friday morning.

So quickly the enemy put doubts into my head

I arranged time off work to take this call so signed off work and sat waiting by the phone for it to ring at 11am. Nothing came. It got to 11:15, and still nothing . . . 11:30, no calls. So quickly the enemy put doubts into my head. I was sure Helen was the one to help me yet she'd not kept her word and called. I was upset with the Lord as I believed He'd directed me to her. I said to Him, *'You wanted me to defend against the divorce, yet You're not helping me. How are You expecting me to do this?'*

I emailed Helen reminding her of our now missed appointment and asked if this would still go ahead another time. That evening she responded. She apologised sincerely stating that she was feeling both under the weather and under pressure, especially after a long day in court the previous day.

She rescheduled to speak to me the next day, a Saturday.

I knew she was the right person to take on this task

During Saturday's call I had the freedom to give her an overview and the context of my situation, making sure I didn't leave out all the Lord had done for Rebecca and me. She was completely onboard with what I had said and appreciated there was a spiritual battle going on. We actually ended up talking a long time about the Lord and His part in our lives. She shared how she prays for each of her clients and has a heart for the oppressed. I knew she was the right person to take on this task and thanked the Lord that He had come through for me again.

The wind blows where it wishes, and you hear the sound of it, but cannot tell where it comes from and where it goes. So is everyone who is born of the Spirit.

John 3:8

25.

Change Is In The Air

I felt dry and quenched in spirit

God had planted me in a new family and a new area. As a group we sought the Lord together regarding building the church and seeking His purposes for the area we were in. As more people joined, we started to outgrow the bungalow venue. The way was made to start fellowshipping on a Sunday in a church building where we had previously held monthly meetings, twenty-five minutes' drive away. It seemed illogical to be travelling this distance each week but it did accommodate for other members who had been travelling a long way, thereby shortening the distance for them.

Knowing what cost and opposition there had been for us all in moving to the area, there was a sense of expectation as to what the Lord would do. With the move to the new building also came gradual changes to the way services were conducted. I found the changes restricted the flow of the Holy Spirit in me yet it was apparent the conviction of the two elders on these matters was unmoving. I felt dry and quenched in spirit and I was not alone in this. Some noted a lack of joy in me. Along with Lydia and Rose, the two ladies I met regularly with to pray, we fasted and interceded until we believed the Lord showed us to stop and not touch this. It was not a battle for us to engage in. Instead, we used our prayer times to worship the Lord more freely.

And she said, 'Let your maidservant find favour in your sight.' So the woman went her way and ate, and her face was no longer sad.

1 Samuel 1:18

26.

So Are My Ways Higher Than Your Ways

It had been at the centre of negative news coverage

I was perplexed at the new emerging direction of the church, viewing it as departing from the original vision of reaching souls in the area God had called us to. Having come into a broad place, I was now finding myself in a place of restriction once more. God was gracious and I had blessed times alone with Him in prayer, worshipping Him often in my home. This led to frequent intermittent fasting until I found myself in a period of complete fasting from food with an increased burden for the lost and evangelising in the area.

I began praying for the lost souls of Leigh Park, the area in Havant Michael had strongly opposed because of its low socio-economic status and bad reputation. In the 1800s it had been home to Leigh Estate, and was described as 'one of the most beautiful spots in the county', encompassing lakes, parks and gardens within a countryside setting. However, during World War Two it was redeveloped as a new suburb for those made homeless in the nearby city of Portsmouth. This allowed for the reconstruction of new roads and parks for Portsmouth following the damage caused by bombing. Post-war, Portsmouth City Council purchased the land and it soon became one of the largest council estates in Europe. More recently it had been at the centre of negative news coverage. Some of the stories included a man who had been set alight on a park bench, a robbery of £100,000 from a local bank and a particularly horrific murder. God was revealing to me His heart and burden over this place and the people.

I had not thought divorce to really be an acceptable option

It came as a surprise to me, then, when the Lord unexpectedly showed me I was not to carry both the burden of Leigh Park and that of the marriage. It was time to lay down the marriage and let go of intercession for Michael. He then gave me the very verse I had rejected almost a year before from the visiting evangelist: *'But if the unbeliever departs, let him depart; a brother or a sister is not under bondage in such cases. But God has called us to peace'* (1 Corinthians 7:15). I suddenly became aware that many of my recent prayers for Michael had come from a place of religiosity; not wanting the shame and stigma of divorce. I had not thought divorce to really be an acceptable option. But now the Lord was showing me He wanted to release me from the bondage and affliction that came through the marriage, calling me to peace. The separation *from* this tie in my life accompanied the directive I was being separated *unto* a service for the Lord. Although Michael had shown no signs of repentance or change, I had not expected to hear this from the Lord. It became clear, however, that I needed to be free from the bondage of Egypt if I was to offer my sacrifice to the Lord in the wilderness. God was permitting a death and severing in this area of my life for me to know the life and empowering of Christ needed to fulfil His calling.

I really was the most unlikely person to go out speaking to people about Christ

I initially kept this to myself but felt led to email the evangelist known to our fellowship and share this burden to witness and how the Lord was leading me. I knew I lacked boldness and was especially weak in this area. I really was the most unlikely person to go out speaking to people about Christ. He graciously encouraged and advised. I apologised for my rejection of the verse he had given the year before, sharing what had come to light regarding this. Having prayed for boldness, the Lord did amazingly provide some opportunities for me to witness but I felt this just to be a foretaste of more to come.

Jesus answered and said to them, 'Those who are well have no need of a physician, but those who are sick. I have not come to call the righteous, but sinners, to repentance.'

Luke 5:31-32

27.

If Benches Could Talk . . .

No . . . not her, Lord . . . Anyone but her

With my increased desire to witness, while walking into town I found myself praying for the Lord to give me an opportunity to speak to someone about Christ. It wasn't long after entering the shopping centre that I noticed in front of me a lady sitting on a bench. She rather abruptly and seemingly out of nowhere produced what looked like a hand-held honker. She blasted this at an innocent man walking by whilst shouting abuse at him! The poor man quickened his pace and did his best to ignore the woman who now had the attention of everyone in the shopping centre. This moment passed as suddenly as it had begun, and she returned to passively sitting on the bench like nothing at all had happened, with everyone else doing the same, going about their business as before. *No . . . not her, Lord . . . Anyone but her.* I began to immediately regret my prayer to the Lord and procrastinated by going into a nearby shop to seek what the Lord wanted me to do.

After delaying and wandering around a shop I had no interest in, I thought I'd go back out again, hoping she'd be gone by now. She was still there. I could have fooled myself into thinking the scene that had played out before had never really happened, as she was now tucking into a sandwich in an ordinary fashion. *Lord, I don't know what you want me to do and I really don't want to speak to this lady.*

After circling around the centre once, I felt the Lord just wanted me to sit next to her. I could do that. It meant her moving her bag so I'd need to ask her if I could sit there. I went up to her and politely asked if I could sit next to her. She obliged and moved her bag for me. Now, sitting on this bench I had no inspiration whatsoever as to what to say to her! On a positive note, at least she was not hurling abuse at me like I knew she was capable of. Nothing I thought to say seemed natural. I believed I was just to sit there and pray. So under my breath I began praying, in English and in tongues. After about five minutes, she unashamedly and ferociously belched and then just walked away!

The Lord was testing my obedience

I never got to speak to her and wondered what that had all been about. Tempting as it was to claim my praying in tongues had seen the deliverance of a demon via this woman's gas release of the upper digestive tract, I had to admit that was a little far-fetched. It was more probable the Lord was testing my obedience and training me in taking these small steps to make way for the Holy Spirit to use me. Her obtrusive belch was, no doubt, just a triumphant response to the sandwich recently consumed. Hopefully, next time I'd open my mouth (with as much ease as this woman had) and the Lord would fill it with His words.

I asked if I could pray for her

My next 'bench' encounter, some weeks later, came more naturally, thanks to the chocolate I'd just bought. Ravenous after my swim, I'd impulsively purchased a pack of Toffifee. I'd recently learnt the small circular inserts on the packaging were for ease of popping out the chocolate. So, keen to try this out, I positioned myself on a bench next to a lady and offered her one, which she very gratefully accepted. This hack worked a little too well and saw the chocolate shoot out at speed, landing somewhere on the bench between us. *I was going to need a little more practice at that.*

This proved to be just the ice breaker needed. We then got talking and she opened up about her social anxiety and how difficult it was to be around people. There was a hint that this may have been caused by some abuse or trauma she'd experienced in the past. I listened sympathetically to her and told her I was a Christian. She had some links to a church and so, before parting, I asked if I could pray for her. She was happy to receive prayer from me and so I hope the Lord used me that day to strengthen and encourage her.

This exchange all happened in the presence of another lady sitting directly behind us on an adjoining bench. I'd hoped I had somehow witnessed to her also.

Inappropriate laughter would at any minute erupt from me

Lydia and I one afternoon decided to walk and pray around Havant shopping centre. Lydia felt led to approach an old man who was playing the public piano there to see if he could play a hymn we could sing to. He whipped out a Billy Graham song book and we attempted to sing along. The old man, whose name was Peter, adopted a unique and interchangeable tempo to his playing that, at times, had Lydia and I scrambling to squeeze in the song words of 'Amazing Grace'. Lost in his own world and perfectly contented, Peter seemed oblivious to this. A couple of songs later, after some sideways glances between Lydia and myself, and with the threat that inappropriate laughter would at any minute erupt from me, we swiftly abandoned the singing. It was probably wishful thinking to believe the quirky timing and fumbling vocals could pass as yet another modern rendition of this hymn. More realistically, we were in danger of discouraging passers-by from depositing in the charity bucket on the piano.

Jesus had saved him from decapitation

Instead, Lydia changed tack and asked Peter if he was a Christian. His face lit up as he began to tell us the story of how, during his time in the Navy, Jesus had saved him from decapitation when he was left hanging off the end of an aircraft carrier! He then beckoned to his wife – a lady very distinctive in her red bobble hat – to come over from a nearby bench. Next to suddenly appear on the scene was their son, who shared how he had been miraculously saved out of alcoholism. What other family members did Peter have stationed in the shopping centre? My eyes scanned around to see who else could be out there. Perhaps a cousin would be signalled over from the nearby balcony. Peter explained that for the last two years they had been going to this shopping centre in order to witness. While he played the piano his family members stationed themselves on benches ready to speak about the Lord to whoever would sit next to them.

A beautiful picture for me of a threefold cord not easily broken

Peter and his wife had a lovely story to tell of how the Lord had brought them together, both initially thinking they were not good enough for one another. Now, here they were unified in marriage but also in ministry. I experienced a brief pang of yearning and envy at what these two had. The union of two souls abandoned to the service of their Saviour was a beautiful picture for me of a threefold cord not easily broken. My own marriage had not reflected such a treasure, and to hope that I could experience such a gift, this side of heaven, was seemingly now unattainable. Yet, just for a moment, to behold it in these two was nonetheless precious. To the natural eye they were perhaps a comical pair; their 'fishing' efforts seemingly futile. To me, they harboured a real treasure that would last into eternity and I would savour that profound illustration.

Lydia, that day, received revelation that we had stepped on another's ground. The Lord already had this ground covered with His saints – Peter, his wife and their son faithfully casting out their nets, drawing in those who were being called. I had discovered that day how the Lord likes to use benches! If the benches in Havant could talk I'm sure they'd have some stories to tell . . .

Most assuredly, I say to you,
when you were younger, you girded yourself and
walked where you wished; but when you are old,
you will stretch out your hands, and another will
gird you and carry you where you do not wish.

John 21:18

28.

One Sows And Another Reaps

I found I just couldn't eat until this task had been discharged

Lydia had known my recent heart to reach the lost but expressed some concern over my fasting in case I was being overly religious about it. This gave opportunity for me to tentatively share that the Lord had told me to let go of Michael. She supported this, believing it to be of the Lord. She shared with me that Stefan had sensed for some time that this was the direction things were heading but they recognised the Holy Spirit needed to be the one to reveal it to me. I knew I had to tell my pastor of this decision to no longer intercede for the marriage but to allow the divorce Michael had initiated to go through. I found I just couldn't eat until this task had been discharged and I ended up fasting over a period of four days until I'd managed to share with him.

I would need to bear any reproach and misunderstanding

It began to dawn on me that I was in the centre of and living out a contentious topic within churches: the matter of divorce. I struggled with feelings of guilt and shame. Some in the church fully supported and understood whilst others remained reserved and cautious, perhaps in silent disapproval. I would need to bear any reproach and misunderstanding from others. I could not condemn people's opinions and religiosity on this as I myself had held their view, but now it appeared the Lord had caused a humbling in me over this matter. He was removing my own judgemental outlook to teach me a lesson necessary to be able to minister to others perhaps in similar situations.

God was writing a different story

There was both a release and a pain in letting go and laying down the marriage: a release, because God was allowing a freedom from the affliction and bondage; a pain, because I had failed to rescue my husband. I had married him with the intention of never parting. Having served in the marriage for thirteen years, it had become my ministry, but now the Lord was telling me my work was done and it was time to let go. Perhaps what I had sown, another would get to reap one day and there was yet an appointed time for his redemption. Nothing is wasted. It wasn't a public ministry reaching crowds of people from a stage for all to observe; it was ministry to just one man. I believe God saw all my works and all that had been sown in tears behind closed doors. I hoped for a reaping in joy and a reward for that done solely unto Him. We are not to grow weary in doing good. My victory, it was turning out, was not to be in the triumph of a restored marriage. God was writing a different story from the one I'd envisaged. My job was to simply trust and obey. My life was not my own.

Now the LORD blessed the latter days of Job more than his beginning.

Job 42:12

29.

Through A Child's Eyes

Daddy would not be coming back to live with us

It pained me knowing Rebecca was the innocent victim in all of this. She loved both myself and her father very much and she did not deserve to grow up without the presence and good modelling of a father and mother in the same household. She visited and spent time with friends in Christian homes where she could observe healthy marriages. I engaged her in discussions around the biblical principles and responsibilities of a husband and wife. Conversations were never forced but flowed freely, usually just over breakfast. The Holy Spirit was faithful to provide opportunities.

Having accepted now that divorce was inevitable and God was permitting it, I approached this difficult subject with Rebecca. I told her that I believed God had shown me that Daddy would not be coming back to live with us but it would be okay because He would take care of us. I shared the verse from 1 Corinthians 7:15 explaining how we had been trapped and exposed to things we shouldn't have, but now God wanted to free us and give us peace. She became a little tearful as she processed this news. The hope she had carried of her daddy returning was not going to materialise. We'd just finished going through the book of Job together and so I reminded her that sometimes things are taken away from us but the story doesn't end there. I encouraged her that God's intentions were to bless us – He had a better plan for us. I reaffirmed the love both Michael and I have for her and the magnitude of God's love for her.

I hoped this biblical foundation would stand her in good stead

After school that day, the first thing Rebecca relayed to me was the lesson she had heard in her school assembly. The theme had been about how sometimes we have our own plans but God's plans can be different and how His ways are always better for us. She said it had made her think of our conversation. God had confirmed to her to trust His way.

Other healthy conversations followed relating to the topic of divorce and I was always surprised at Rebecca's level of emotional maturity, insight and wisdom. She could recognise fear was a root of some of the irrational behaviour and control perpetrated by her father. All the while she would be obedient to Michael and not trigger any areas of insecurity or fear, they would retain a lovely relationship. However, if he didn't change I knew the time may come, as her faith grew, that her decisions and freedom to serve God could unsettle him. He was at times paranoid over her safety and fearful of any kind of harm against her. The only way he knew to manage this was to impose and enforce rules, through control and fear, as a way of trying to reduce anxiety for himself. All I could do was ensure she had sound biblical teaching and a relationship with God. Should she ever face such challenges in her future, I hoped this biblical foundation would stand her in good stead. It has been my prayer that she would choose obedience to God above all else, without fear and knowing God will always provide a way of escape. I did not want her to come under the same bondage Michael was under.

God would still keep one mighty sower at work there

Although I had been withdrawn from the mission field of Michael's heart, God would still keep one mighty sower at work there. This little girl with a big faith. Let us not underestimate a child-like faith but rather seek to preserve it. At age seven Rebecca had written the following prayer to her Abba Father in heaven beseeching Him to rescue the soul of her daddy on earth:

To GOD
I pray for daddy

Because I love him and I
Wont want to see him die in
hell God Soften his heart
to turn to God love me and
you. and use him as a tool
to preach your Word help
him to learn at church and
have faith in you and help
his family too because I can't

help Because my strenth belief
and thas worthy comes Stay
You Lord

115

/ No Wone can be better at Saving than
you oh Lord worry help daddy to

become a follower of God Lord jesus
Chist that died on a cross for
evrey one girls boys gentiles.
Jus and ~~rich~~ rich poor people
evreyone men Woman evreyone
Like daddy even people we
dont Know Like even people against
us Like murders thiefs robers
help them to trust in you too GOD

HOLY GOD
ALMIGHTY
Are Savior AND Lord

116

Rest in the LORD, and wait patiently for Him;
do not fret because of him who prospers in his way,
because of the man who brings wicked schemes to pass.

Psalm 37:7

30.

Let Patience Have Its Perfect Work

There were moments that really tested me

I wrote to Helen advising her of the new direction I felt the Lord was taking me in and she said my email had really touched her. She completely understood this leading from the Lord. I had done all I could to defend the marriage but as long as Michael remained hardened, divorce was always going to be the outcome. I now viewed the divorce as a means the Lord had permitted to free me for His purposes. I was keen to see it pushed through so I could move on.

However, there were moments that really tested me. Sometimes I wouldn't get replies to emails and days would turn into weeks and then into months of no communication from Helen. Quite often our prayer group would need to bring this before the Lord so that my case would be brought to her attention above all the other cases she was having to deal with. Often there were immediate results in the natural following our wrestling through in prayer, showing us there was contending to do in the spiritual realm on this matter. As someone who likes to keep my word, be on time and be efficient, I needed a real grace from the Lord to make allowances for others weaker in this area. I knew that any of Helen's silences were due to her being extremely hard pressed and busy.

I don't like patience being worked in as it takes too long!

The delays were sometimes excruciatingly agonising but it was all out of my control. I really wanted an end and conclusion to it all rather than the perpetual uncertainty of our future provision. When I sought the Lord over this He revealed He was working patience into me. Without realising the irony of my statement until I'd said it, my response was, *'I don't like patience being worked in as it takes too long!'* The Lord was clearly highlighting that just because He gives me a Word or reveals a direction, it does not mean it will happen immediately. I was sometimes impatient in waiting for things to come at God's allotted time, so needed this virtue developed in me.

I knew he had pursued a relationship with the Irish woman

When Helen did make contact she was efficient and handled matters well. She initiated a financial disclosure from both parties. There were no assets or savings held by either of us except for the property I owned as a buy-to-let. I depended on the income from renting this property to afford my current accommodation. Michael's bank statements revealed he'd been to Ireland so I knew he had pursued a relationship with the Irish woman. This was no surprise to me and caused no reaction or any kind of stirring within me. I felt completely emotionally detached. I told Helen I did not need her to pursue any kind of maintenance payment or income from Michael. My only desire was that he would stop trying to take what I had worked for – essentially my provision for Rebecca. My greatest desire was to be free from this affliction.

****

O captive daughter
Loose yourself from the bonds of your affliction
O reproached daughter
Your faith has healed you of your affliction

**Put on strength
You will be redeemed**

**Behold, I will do a new thing
Now it shall spring forth
I will even make a road in the wilderness
And rivers in the desert
Rivers in the desert**

Desolate daughter
I've sought you, you'll no longer be forsaken
Rejected daughter
Hephzibah will be your name, not forsaken

Shall you not know it, nor perceive?
Blessed are those who have not seen, yet believe.

****

LYRICS FROM 'RIVERS IN THE DESERT'
2023 SONG BY HANNAH

As they ministered to the Lord and fasted, the Holy Spirit said, 'Now separate to Me Barnabas and Saul for the work to which I have called them.'

Acts 13:2

31.

Rivers In The Desert

Now it shall spring forth

I sensed the Lord was going to do a new thing in my life and I would be entering into a new season. He impressed upon me the following verse from Isaiah:

Behold, I will do a new thing, now it shall spring forth; shall you not know it? I will even make a road in the wilderness and rivers in the desert.

Isaiah 43:19

There was a quickening from the Lord. The things He was revealing to me and a few other co-labourers in the Lord were not on the same trajectory as the church's. I felt like there was more God wanted to do but I was restricted in service and growth under the new direction of the church.

Obed Edom

At this time Lydia shared that God had impressed upon her the words 'Obed Edom' one morning and that He was showing her that her family were to begin meeting in their home. The story of Obed Edom is found in 2 Samuel 6. After the Ark of the Covenant (representing God's glory) had been incorrectly transported it was brought to Obed Edom's house for three months, bringing blessing upon the household. Knowing I was not in the right place and in need of my own reconfiguration, this witnessed with me. It was then that Lydia shared Stefan had already received the directive from the Lord to become a pastor. I knew then this was the opening I had needed and where I was to be. The Lord had been preparing me for the calling to this house church to fulfil my service to Him. I was to fellowship in and witness from the area in which I was living. This presented me with another separation I had not foreseen.

It seemed two separate paths had emerged

I viewed the people I had been fellowshipping with as my family. They had been there for me and journeyed with me, helping bear the burden of all I had experienced. Now the Lord was requiring a parting. It seemed two separate paths had emerged and this would be another cost of following Christ. If the past three years had taught me anything, it was to be quick to obey the Lord when He calls and remain close to Him above all else. I had known a giving and taking away of those I love but knew nothing could separate me from the love of Christ. I had to go with Him no matter the cost. I was reminded of the following song lyrics, which were written two years before this separation. I became aware I was coming into the fulfilment of these words:

****

Arise, O soul,
The Shepherd's calling you
Come out from them
To a pasture new

The sound of many waters
Or still and small
When you hear His voice
Take heed to His call

Have you counted the cost of knowing Christ?
Your life will be lost for this new life
Count all things as loss
Take up your cross
To be after God's own heart
The things of this world, depart.

Be as shrewd as snakes
Like doves be innocent
Sheep among wolves
You have been sent

Clothed in His armour
With the word as your sword
Knowing an inheritance for your work
Will be your reward

Speak in the light
What you hear in the dark
Do not fear, for on you
He has placed His mark

Arise, O soul,
The Shepherd's calling you.

****

LYRICS FROM 'THE SHEPHERD'S CALLING YOU'
2021 SONG BY HANNAH

To the weak I became as weak, that I might win the weak. I have become all things to all men, that I might by all means save some. Now this I do for the gospel's sake, that I may be partaker of it with you.

1 Corinthians 9:22-23

32.

Here Am I! Send Me.

God was showing me; to serve amongst the despised, poor, rejected and reproached

One morning, soon after, I woke with the unction to write to the elders and sensitively share my revelation; that God was calling me to leave the church. I needed to fulfil the vision God was showing me; to serve amongst the despised, poor, rejected and reproached in the area I was living. It became clear to me I had needed to become these very things in order to be able to minister the same mercy and compassion of Christ I had received. My desire was to see souls freed, receiving a deep knowledge and experience of God's saving grace.

Time was short and the days getting darker

Having prayed faithfully with Lydia and Rose each week for the last three years into the atrocity of abortion, I knew that the Lord was calling us into a practical work to function from the fellowship. God had moved both Rose and myself especially to this area in which Lydia was already residing, and had been training and preparing all three of us to serve Him here. Our burden was to intercede and be a voice for the voiceless, particularly relating to the issue of abortion but also for other vulnerable members of society. In this day and for a time at least, it seemed God was allowing grace – a restraining of judgement by raising up those who would intercede for righteousness. No more did discussions of doctrines and the approbation of theologians within the walls of church suffice; I was itching to get to where God purposed me to be and serve Him. Time was short and the days getting darker, yet the fields were white for harvest:

127

Also I heard the voice of the Lord, saying:
'Whom shall I send, and who will go for Us?'
Then I said, 'Here am I! Send me.'

Isaiah 6:8

For which of you, intending to build a tower,
does not sit down first and count the cost,
whether he has enough to finish it – lest,
after he has laid the foundation, and is not able to
finish, all who see it begin to mock him saying,
'This man began to build and was not able to finish'?

Luke 14:28-30

33.

Counting The Cost

God had shown us there was to be no delay in parting

All earlier zeal, enthusiasm and hopefulness for this 'new life' and birth of ministry very soon dwindled when it became apparent my leaving, and that of a few others, was not to be viewed in the same light by those we were parting from. The honesty of my heartfelt letter, whilst expressing sincere love (it had been checked by another pastor before sending), prompted a focus from the church leaders on the internal aspects and doctrine within the church that I'd struggled with. The calling and the reason why I was departing had been overlooked. There was no acknowledgement that the Lord had called us to minister in the area we were living in. Instead, it was perceived that leaving was a sign of disobedience and betrayal towards those we had fellowshipped with.

God had shown us there was to be no delay in parting, yet the caution I received from the elders was not to rush. Therefore I agreed to seek counsel from other godly men known to us for my own covering and out of submission to this process that seemed to be required of me. I thought by jumping through these hoops I could obtain the blessing and recognition that I'd been desiring for a peaceable send off. Would I be able to convince the leaders I was not deceived and not simply following the dictates of my own heart?

Friends and family were diminishing, divorce loomed and affliction was increasing

This same month, May 2023, saw my thirty-sixth birthday come and go. Rebecca joined me on my bed for the grand opening of my cards. I had to laugh as I beheld the four birthday cards set out in front of me. It was going to be a job stringing this out. There was at least one price sticker to slowly peel off the back of a card so that helped prolong the 'event'. *Cards had gone up in price*. I remembered how Michael's large family would each give me cards but now, of course, I had no contact with them. That included my seven nieces and nephews of whom I had been fond. His family would have been fed whatever narrative Michael was choosing to give them.

On this day, I afforded a brief reflection of my life so far. Through the lens of self-pity I could see I had little to boast about naturally speaking – friends and family were diminishing, divorce loomed and affliction was increasing. At this rate, by forty I'd have no cards and there was no telling what horrendous circumstances could be upon me. This time for me went slowly. Potentially I still had a lot of life yet to live. I would need all the help and grace I could get from the Lord to endure whatever still lay ahead!

However, having removed the self-pity spectacles, any woes paled in comparison to my relationship with the Lord and the joy found in knowing Him. I could have all the friends, family, cards and material blessings this world could offer, yet, without Jesus I would be hopelessly empty. Take the world but give me Jesus!

*By long forbearance a ruler is persuaded,
and a gentle tongue breaks a bone.*

Proverbs 25:15

34.

For Do I Now Persuade Men, Or God?

I was limited as to whom I could ask for help

Knowing very few people outside of the church in a position to weigh what the Lord had been showing me, I was limited as to whom I could ask for help. Mark, the pastor who had checked my letter and was well known to Stefan and Lydia, was already supportive of the direction the Lord had shown them. A visit to him offered encouragement, prayer and support. His own church had started in a similar way and he had felt such joy in his spirit when Stefan and Lydia had told him of Living Stones – the name of the new church God was beginning. While visiting Mark and his family, he'd shared with us a passage from Ezra 7, stating that as the Lord had decreed it, it would be done and provided for. To me, he specifically said, '*And the King has paid for it.*' This seemed obscure and almost cryptic, yet noteworthy, and I sensed just to hold onto this Word.

The elders expressed concern with me approaching someone who was just going to be favourable so I identified two more godly men known to them. One responded via email and the other requested a phone call. Leading up to the phone call, I'd felt apprehensive that this person could take a harsh approach and so I asked a few people to pray prior to the conversation. One of them sent me the following quote:

Letting people be wrong about you or a situation while keeping your peace and focus is the most misunderstood power move you'll ever make.

Morgan Richard Olivier

Sure enough, the call proved to be just this test for me. Much of our conversation was fine – there was a shared acknowledgement of not being introspective in order to reach people for Christ, as time is short. However, he had called and spoken to one of the elders prior to speaking to me and so conducted the call from a certain viewpoint. I was disappointed that he had gone to man first and not God for discernment. Previously I had shared with him in good faith something of my situation and personal life, but now, his narrative and perception of me and my life was far from reality.

I'd received an honest opinion at least

The call turned into what felt like a job interview – one where the interviewer does not want you to get the job! Through questioning he implied that I was being rebellious against authority with the suspicion that overbearing women were at play, that I was going where I thought the grass was greener (where I'd have no covering), and that based on his experience of divorced women, perhaps I'd become hard-hearted towards men, with divorce being my quest for freedom and independence.

I did my best to defend myself and answer his questions honestly, showing no disdain. I knew to graciously endure harsh misjudgement of my character, acknowledging it was me who had approached him and opened myself up to this. He applied a passage of scripture to me from Numbers 12, where Miriam criticised Moses, becoming leprous as a result. Although this was not his intention, it triggered memories of how Michael would use scriptures to exercise misplaced discipline and impose the fear that I was under God's wrath and judgement. Making no comment, I thanked him for sharing and said I would consider this. I asked if I could pray for him at the end of the call and he prayed for me also. I was grateful for the time he had given me and couldn't deny I'd received an honest opinion at least.

I suffered, daily, a mental vexing

This wasn't quite the encouragement into the calling I was hoping for and in the days and weeks that followed, I suffered, daily, a mental vexing. I'd endured the hour phone call as well as a two-and-half-hour meeting alone with the elders prior to that. Any good intentions in what had been said were drowned out by the negative words spoken over me. These were people I sincerely respected and had trusted and I was deeply wounded. Even prior to becoming divorced, the very labels and stigma of divorce I had wanted to avoid had been placed upon me. The enemy was not original in his methods – heaping upon me the familiar accusations that I was disobedient and deceived. This time, instead of the accusations coming through Michael, they had come through other men.

It felt like God was bringing me to a low place

In addition to this, in my weakened state I was susceptible to the guilt placed upon me when addressed by a couple of people to consider the impact my leaving would have on others. The weight of being misunderstood and absence of anyone coming to my defence became a heavy burden. It felt like God was bringing me to a low place of being weak and helpless. Hurt and injustice consumed me; I was just a single mother trying to respond in obedience to the call of God yet there was so much attack against this desire to serve Him. I couldn't break free. Had I purely been a hard-hearted rebellious woman seeking to overrule man's authority I'm sure I would have coped better in this situation. But the truth was, I was especially sensitive to all that had occurred and had needed a male to stand in the gap to shield something of what I was now experiencing. I wanted vindication, recognition and justice. I questioned God, why He wasn't defending the weak. Was I not the woman trying to bring an offering before the Lord whilst the disciples criticised her? Jesus said, *'Let her alone. Why do you trouble her? She has done a good work for Me'* (Mark 14:6).

Deliver yourself like a gazelle from the hand of the hunter,
and like a bird from the hand of the fowler.

Proverbs 6:5

Most assuredly, I say to you, unless a grain of wheat falls into the ground and dies, it remains alone; but if it dies, it produces much grain. He who loves his life will lose it, and he who hates his life in this world will keep it for eternal life. If anyone serves Me, let him follow Me; and where I am, there My servant will be also. If anyone serves Me, him My Father will honour.

John 12:24-26

35.

Death

I was worse off than someone on benefits

At the same time, divorce proceedings began to take their toll. I had to face the reality that with an impending tripling of the mortgage rate on the property I owned, along with Michael's demand for money, I would not have enough finances for Rebecca's and my needs. Our expenses were soon to be greater than our income. My mortgage broker, after looking at my finances, told me I was worse off than someone on benefits. Ironically, the time actually did come, some months later, when I would find myself short of money for my upcoming rent payment with no choice but to apply for benefits. These pressures, along with the mental vexation that came with trying to leave the church, meant I didn't have the capacity to deal with everything or focus on my job. I knew I needed to prioritise Rebecca and ensure I was in good health for her sake. I was signed off sick for two to three weeks to allow breathing space, time with God and time to complete some pressing administrative tasks.

I was seeking affirmation and recognition of God's calling

I told the Lord I felt like the man in the good Samaritan story, just trying to get from 'A' to 'B' but now half-dead, wounded on the roadside with people passing by. I started hoping that the third response I was waiting for would, like the good Samaritan, come to my rescue and I would have someone stand in the gap and defend where others had failed. I was seeking affirmation and recognition of God's calling.

God had been waiting for me to reach that place of surrender

Time passed by as I waited for the response from the final person asked to weigh the information detailing the calling God had put upon me. I despairingly sought the Lord, desperate now for a positive response and a severing from the church so I could move on. My prayers reached a point where I said to God, '*Lord, not my will but Yours. Even if no one backs me, if no one defends me, if no one recognises this call . . . I still choose to follow You. I don't need man's affirmation or recognition, You are all that matters.*' I repented of needing man's approval.

Literally seconds after I had prayed that prayer, the email response came through on my phone. God had been waiting for me to reach that place of surrender. The third person wrote sensitively, giving sound advice but also raising a number of cautions, including not rushing, not neglecting care of Rebecca due to ministry and that, because of my past experiences, I may not be ready to minister. I was now able to summarise all responses to the elders in what I hoped was a humble and loving letter. I thanked them for their input and love towards me and my daughter but stated it was by faith that I was choosing to leave, without further delay, to follow the Lord. I trusted Him for all the enabling as, just as people had pointed out, on paper, and under man's scrutiny and expectations, I didn't qualify.

I'd got the wrong story

I revisited the good Samaritan story with the Lord asking why no one came to my rescue. He told me I'd got the wrong story. This was about the cross. The whole point was that I die. There was going to be no rescue. I was to die to self-preservation, seeking approval from man, the need to defend myself and the desire to be vindicated. It all had to be put to death.

The final correspondence from the leaders to the few of us that had left stated that biblical protocol hadn't been adhered to, people had been hurt and confused and therefore, as such, fellowship with us in the immediate future would be difficult. The closer Jesus got to the cross, the fewer people He had around Him. I had to go forward with the Lord on my own again.

I'd been in a similar place before but it was a different pain having been rejected and misunderstood by brothers and sisters in Christ. The 'new life' I'd been zealous for now seemed very distant. I would learn that the empowering and anointing obtained from 'new life' cannot come without first passing through death. Death – this breaking and crushing of me, felt uncomfortable, agonising, lonely, relentless and painful and I wasn't the only one in the group having to go through this. The others, too, had paid a great price. We were now alone with very few in support of us.

The Lord stripped me of my car

To make matters worse, my car broke down needing a new clutch, which I didn't have enough money for. The Lord stripped me of my car for four weeks until, by the generosity of my new fellowship and my parents, I was given enough for it to be repaired.

Rather abruptly, contact from a number of people had ceased. I no longer saw people I was used to seeing throughout the week, and friendships that had been there within the church didn't remain outside the church. I was removed from an email newsletter I was subscribed to without understanding why at the time. I felt prompted by the Lord that my response to this needed to be to anonymously give some money, out of the little I had, to their ministry and pray blessing over it. I was also to continually pray forgiveness and blessing over those who didn't feel able to contact me or maintain a friendship with me anymore. Not only was this right to do, it was necessary to keep bitterness away and enable healing. The Lord's ways are higher and His wisdom greater than our own. He supplied all the grace and forgiveness I needed.

It was the 'guarding' of the heart that was necessary

I was bothered by the concept that loving and trusting others inevitably led to pain when betrayed or judged by them. Was my heart too soft and tender? Should I try and toughen up and harden it to avoid this kind of hurt? I believe the Lord answered that it needed to remain soft and loving but it was the 'guarding' of the heart that was necessary, not a hardening of it. What seemed a harsh cutting off from people had really been the Lord closing doors of contact out of protection. He was establishing boundaries between myself and others who, for this season, were not to continue with me in this journey.

And the peace of God, which surpasses all understanding,
will guard your hearts and minds through Christ Jesus.

Philippians 4:7

'The King has paid for it'

In light of this and after a time of prayer, I knew I needed to release those who had committed to offer financial assistance for the solicitor fees (which had not yet been determined). Mark's words echoed in my head, 'The King has paid for it.' *But if I let go of this offer, I'll have no way of paying and the process will not be able to continue. I'll be without Helen, undefended and unable to break free.* This required a step of faith from me. Was I going to believe the King has paid for it before seeing how? I emailed the people and by faith told them that the Lord had provided for me, and that I no longer would require their kind offer to help. I now felt more vulnerable than before but this was a severing the Lord had required.

A few days later, without my prompting or disclosing, I received an offer from elsewhere to pay for solicitor's fees. The King had paid for it. *Thank You, Lord.*

*And another also said, 'Lord, I will follow You,
but let me first go and bid them farewell
who are at my house.' But Jesus said to him,
'No one, having put his hand to the plough,
and looking back, is fit for the kingdom of God.'*

Luke 9:61-62

36.

Looking Forward

Huddled in the lounge of the pastor's home

S evering from the church came at a great cost and the affliction was extremely difficult to bear. However, it gave us hope that the Lord was in this work – otherwise the enemy would not have given it so much attention.

The new church fellowship started on Sunday 4th June 2023 and consisted of three men, four women, and three children. That day we huddled in the lounge of the pastor's home, in the centre of Leigh Park. Our name, Living Stones Fellowship, now seemed especially fitting. We had become those rejected by people but chosen by God:

Coming to Him as to a living stone, rejected indeed by men, but chosen by God and precious, you also, as living stones, are being built up a spiritual house, a holy priesthood, to offer up spiritual sacrifices acceptable to God through Jesus Christ.

1 Peter 2:4-5

Our meetings were blessed and we were led to intercede in the area. One Sunday, we walked past the local stream, stopping there specifically to pray before moving on to a road we believed was going to be a focal point for this work. There were strongholds that needed to be broken and enemy territory to be regained for the purpose of rebuilding for Christ.

A body found in the stream

That evening, we received news from Rose that her husband Richard had fallen badly. It transpired that he had broken his neck and subsequently would be hospitalised. During the same night I was awoken by Rebecca coming into my room saying she'd been sick. It turned into a restless night as her bout of sickness lasted until dawn. In the morning we heard there had been a body found in the stream – the very same area we'd prayed in the day before. The enormity of the spiritual battle for this area dawned on me. Our prayers had clearly aggravated the enemy.

Thankfully (and miraculously) Richard was not paralysed after his accident and Rebecca's sickness episode subsided. We did learn, however, that the body of the man found in the stream was the result of murder. The wickedness in the area of Leigh Park had reached the attention of God and His eyes were running to and fro, looking for loyal hearts to rise up and intercede. By all accounts, we were an unlikely bunch! Despite being aware of our limitations, we were willing to stand in the gap and seek the Lord's mercy and healing for the land.

Not feeling His presence

Some of our group shared in the struggle – feeling of a lack of closeness to the Lord. I believed He was testing us, like a parent who leaves a child alone and watches from a distance to see how obediently they respond. Would we obey, even when we were not feeling His presence? I also recalled Jesus being forsaken on the cross. The absence of 'feeling' the presence and nearness of the Lord was part of the 'death' and breaking we needed to pass through. It was not a sign of disobedience. When Jesus in obedience hung on the cross, He suffered the agonising separation from the Father. Yet, this was fulfilment of the will of God. We are not to always attribute a feeling of distance from the Lord as being outside of His will.

****

When in the mist and fog of sorrow and pain
And Jesus we cannot see
Yearning to hear His voice of comfort and know
He has not forsaken thee

Had we foreseen the wounds in the house of friends
'Not these shoes,' our cry would be
Though mark a track of faith, that tempts a man's praise
Where they rub, men cannot see

But we don't lose heart, this one test to afford;
Believing in the land we'll see, the goodness of the Lord
To the upward call, our praises we will bring
What was held dear, we leave behind
With a hundredfold to win
Lay down our lives, then life we find
With a hundredfold to win

Broken by love displayed at Golgotha hill
Through death is now our hard way
Misunderstood, this love, that bears all man's scorn
Serving those who can't repay

Humble yourselves under the mighty hand of God
And He will exalt you in due time

****

LYRICS FROM 'A HUNDREDFOLD TO WIN'
2023 SONG BY HANNAH

For who has despised the day of small things?
For these seven rejoice to see the plumb line in the
hand of Zerubbabel. They are the eyes of the LORD,
which scan to and fro throughout the whole earth.

Zechariah 4:10

37.

Faithful In The Small Things

I was actually reaping in a field

One night I was reminded of a specific verse from the book of Ruth, which the Lord had given me back in October 2022, almost a year before:

Let your eyes be on the field which they reap, and go after them. Have I not commanded the young men not to touch you? And when you are thirsty, go to the vessels and drink from what the young men have drawn.

Ruth 2:9

At the time I knew this verse had been quickened to me but was unsure of the application, so I jotted it down in my journal. Ruth, a Moabite woman married into an Israelite family and converted to Judaism. After the death of all the male members of the family, she vows to stay with her mother-in-law Naomi. Poverty stricken, Naomi decides to return to her homeland, to the town of Bethlehem, with the hope of a better future. Ruth forsakes her life in Moab to loyally follow Naomi, declaring, *'For wherever you go, I will go'* (Ruth 1:16).

Ruth begins to work gleaning in the field of Naomi's relative Boaz. Now, like Ruth, I was actually reaping in a field! I'd met some people from another fellowship who had a vision for working the land. I joined them on occasions, sowing and harvesting in their field. I found myself awake that night with God revealing to me the similarities I shared with the narrative of Ruth in the Bible. In obedience to the Spirit's leading, Rebecca and I had also moved house, leaving much behind yet finding refuge under the wings of the Lord (Ruth 2:12). He'd been faithful to deliver Rebecca and me from an untenable situation, moving us suddenly to a place I knew little about in order to commit to a work there.

I was free from labels

As a 'foreigner' or an outsider to their fellowship and their field, I received unearned acceptance and favour. The pastor and his wife, like Boaz, showed kindness and generosity towards me. There was something freeing being amongst those who knew nothing of my affliction and sorrow of the past few years. I was simply known as 'Hannah who moved to Havant and is part of a small fellowship there'. I was free from labels, whether that be 'powerless victim' at one end of the spectrum or 'hard-hearted divorcee' at the other end. Man's scrutiny and misjudgements of my character were kept at a distance. The dramas I'd faced and journey I'd been on were unknown here. I wondered how Ruth's departure to new pastures (Israel) was perceived by her fellow Moabites and whether her obedience to the Lord was misunderstood and criticised by them. Was she exposed to opinions of others that she was destitute, unworthy and inadequate to be used by the Lord? Was she viewed as deceived and hard-hearted for leaving? To some she would have seemed foolish, but others would have recognised her faithfulness to follow Naomi (who can be viewed as a picture of the Holy Spirit in this narrative).

God can anoint land to heal us

Simply working the land proved medicinal. Of course it involved getting my hands dirty, but the greatest misfortune I can recall was getting a potato stuck on the end of my gardening fork and toppling when pulling out a weed – nothing to write home about! It was a very welcome change to past dramas I was used to. Who'd have thought such monotonous work could be the remedy to healing wounds? I experienced such contentment while labouring in the peaceful setting of this field, at the same time reaping some provision for myself and Rebecca. In our fellowship we'd prayed for the Lord to heal the land of Leigh Park but I never stopped to think how God can anoint land to heal us. I had always pitied Ruth having to labour for her and Naomi's provision, but I now wondered if she too found solace and healing from her pain within the protection of Boaz's field. To the onlooker Ruth and Naomi would have appeared poor and destitute, with the hope of a better life seemingly unattainable. However, this is just where the Lord would have them. I was convinced this 'safe field', a place of healing and strengthening after recent trauma, was, for now, the place where God would have me. Simply being faithful in the small things would reap its reward.

What 'new-borns' would God trust me to handle for the advancement of His kingdom?

I pondered the role of 'Boaz' in the narrative of Ruth. Boaz is a picture of Christ – the kinsman redeemer. He protected and accepted the weak, showing kindness and compassion. This was also something of God's directive for Living Stones Fellowship.

The field, for me, represented an intermediate place where restoration was not the ultimate goal or the final destination. Instead, it was at the place of restoration, where Ruth gleaned, she was ready to be found and brought into God's eternal purposes. She had been faithful and would soon be entrusted with more; a baby, that would form part of the lineage of Christ. What 'new-borns' would God trust me to handle for the advancement of His kingdom? I wanted to be found by Christ at His coming as a faithful and virtuous bride, reaping for His kingdom.

I no longer sought vindication

Ruth's decision and commitment to follow Naomi eventually led to her redemption and vindication, but perhaps these were really just by-products of her ultimate aim; to bring glory to God and minister to Him. I no longer sought vindication but was perfectly content ministering to the Lord, unseen. I knew I was where I should be and being in the will of God afforded such a valuable peace. For now I was to let my eyes be on the field; faithful and hardworking in the small things and knowing the Lord's favour upon me. Like Ruth, it was in this place I received protection with free and accessible refreshment to draw from.

God had wholly preserved Rebecca and me; healing us from much of the affliction. There was no going back to the land of Moab, with the subjugation of false gods. Instead, stopping at Bethlehem – the 'house of bread' – was necessary for our nourishment. I needed to patiently allow the Lord to accomplish His inward work in me. Not only was I out of Moab but, one by one, any weeds of Moab could be taken out of me, allowing room for a healthy crop to thrive.

Now there was a long war between the house of Saul and the house of David. But David grew stronger and stronger, and the house of Saul grew weaker and weaker.

2 Samuel 3:1

38.

From Strength To Strength

A generation fed with lies

Having lost the support and contact from many of those who had previously been close, there had been an immediate isolation and a journey of grief to traverse. I would often walk alone praying in the roads of Leigh Park and around where I lived. This produced many opportunities to witness and I felt a greater freedom to talk to people. God really reinvigorated me during these times and sometimes I wondered if He fashioned these opportunities more to encourage me than for any other reason. I developed a heart for the youth, who were generally softer and more receptive to the Word of God. It felt like they were a generation fed with lies and lacking any hope and future.

He has paid for it all

One such encounter occurred at my local convenience store. As I waited for Rebecca to be dropped off by Michael, my eyes were drawn to two loitering youths. It transpired that they were brother and sister, fifteen and twelve years old, respectively. They had been banned from the shop for stealing but were allowed inside with a responsible adult. Somehow, I ended up accompanying them into the store. The 'important' items they had been waiting to purchase were of course located in the sweet aisle. I watched bemused at their efforts to see how many packets of sweets they could buy with the change they had. Taking pity on them, I interjected with some helpful maths, which sadly for them resulted in returning at least one desired packet of sweets to the shelf. That was the first time I was able to share the gospel with these two siblings.

God graciously orchestrated further encounters with them, allowing me to develop the conversations around God. I couldn't help warming to these two and our fellowship committed to praying for them. They showed an interest to coming to church with Tiffany asking, *'Do we need to pay?'* How I yearned for them to truly comprehend that Jesus has paid. He has paid for it all. On the cross at Calvary.

Freely received and freely given

I was learning the importance of being ready in season and out of season (2 Timothy 4:2). With this in mind, another opportunity presented itself to share the gospel with three young girls around the age of ten. They were sitting on the roadside outside a block of flats, attempting to sell shells. It was so heart-warming to see their receptiveness after I shared the gospel with them. I asked if they wanted to say a prayer with me where they would say sorry for their sins and ask Jesus and the Holy Spirit into their lives. They did. Only God knew their hearts and what would become of that encounter.

Before I left, and much to their delight, I bought an overpriced shell from them, making a mental note to dispose of this amongst all the other freely accessible shells when next at the beach. I hoped they would value more what I had freely received and freely given to them.

I still needed further training and wisdom in the area of witnessing

Interestingly, and perhaps almost just as importantly, were the opportunities the Lord blocked. In my enthusiasm sometimes I would try to create my own opportunities. I remember one time going to a café with Rebecca, positioning ourselves specifically outside where I could view passers-by and wait for opportunities to speak to someone. I was keen to speak to someone that day. Quite suddenly, and out of nowhere, a gust of wind blew, making it impossible to remain outside – things were blowing about the table and our hair blowing in our faces. Reluctantly, Rebecca and I moved indoors to a window seat. From my seat, looking outside I saw a man with no shirt on, holding an empty bottle. He was looking particularly agitated, pacing about, shouting at times. He hadn't been there just a few seconds prior and yet now there he was! I couldn't believe I'd narrowly missed this opportunity. I was desperate to get out and talk to him. However, I couldn't leave Rebecca in the café on her own.

Despite my frustration, I knew in my heart God had purposely moved Rebecca and me indoors for our protection. I acknowledged God had shown Himself as a protective covering for us that day. He taught me that I still needed further training and wisdom in the area of witnessing. I recalled the time I'd very reluctantly, and with much persuasion from the Holy Spirit, eventually approached the lady with the 'honker' on the bench. Now here I was desperate to get to this agitated man, who most likely was under the influence of drugs or alcohol, and the Holy Spirit was having to restrain me! Only by the grace of God had I come a long way in overcoming the fear of man. However, discernment was still developing in me.

A little green shoot had broken through hard soil

In addition to witnessing and my time at the allotment, I set my face towards being faithful in and stewarding other 'small things' the Lord had entrusted me with. This included the spiritual teaching and training of Rebecca, writing and sharing songs, serving in worship and Sunday school and attending pro-life displays, in which I had now become a team leader. Little by little I felt the Lord renewing my joy, breathing new life into me and restoring my strength. My singing voice was strengthening as was an inward spiritual voice. Where I had previously been silenced – either externally or because of my own fear of man – I now experienced liberty and a boldness arising from within. It was as if a little green shoot had broken through hard soil, bursting forth to now appear above the ground. I saw light and could feel the warmth of the sun upon me. Had I been planted in the wrong place, the conditions would have delayed or hindered this development. But as such, the gardener had known exactly where to plant me for a prosperous growth. I detected a passion for Christ kindling within me, untameable and uncontainable. From whence had this come? Certainly not from me. It was uncomfortably not very 'British'! A righteousness had come forth as brightness and my salvation as a lamp that burns (Isaiah 62:1-2).

Doors I wasn't expecting started opening

Doors I wasn't expecting started opening and new contacts had emerged. Some invitations to serve elsewhere at other churches and events presented themselves to us and a complimentary two-course dinner unexpectedly came my way, which I wasn't going to turn down! I received encouragement regarding how my songs had ministered to people, even acting as a catalyst for healing in one particular person's life.

Of course, battles were still ever present – there was a three-week period in which the property I rented needed serious DIY remedial work having been left in this sorry state by the tenant. Yet what I witnessed God do through the church was astounding. I was given money by those with little money. Those with little time freely gave time. Those not in the best of health helped labour with me until the work was complete. The grace and compassion of God through these members not only touched me but served as a witness to unsaved family members and the neighbours in that community who would see us tirelessly working together.

I possessed a peace within me

It was now ten months since I had received the letter from Michael's solicitor demanding £30,000, and my response letter was finally being sent. Helen had written a good reply which clearly outlined the facts and exposed the real futility of what Michael was doing. She identified his demand as further control and manipulation and that we would not be 'bowing down' to this. We would be offering nothing and requesting to take nothing. Helen was confident that this was highly unlikely to go to court as the expense of this for him would exceed the value of what he was trying to gain. She told me a judge presented with all the facts would ensure this asset (the property) would justly remain with me as it was essential provision for Rebecca and me. I now just had to await their response and hope this would reach its conclusion soon. I possessed a peace within me and a contentment to patiently wait for God's ordained time. I felt able to continue in my pursuit of serving the Lord even before there was any closure in this area of my life. God had shown me His grace was not restricted to certain places or circumstances in order to be effectual for Him. To have excused myself from being an ambassador for Christ on the grounds that the divorce was still unresolved, would be doing myself and God a disservice.

So he went to him and bandaged his wounds, pouring on oil and wine; and he set him on his own animal, brought him to an inn, and took care of him.

Luke 10:34

39.

Oil And Wine

I feared integrity in this matter was being taken from me

Whilst I never doubted the Holy Spirit's leading and that the decisions I'd made were in obedience to Him, there needed to be a reconciliation between my experience of the Holy Spirit and the Word of God. For the Holy Spirit and the Word of God can never be in contradiction or disunity. I was never comfortable knowing I would become a divorcee, and even less comfortable about becoming the subject of a contentious issue within the church. It had never been my desire to be any kind of voice in this matter. God brought this to my door and led me down the path of His choosing, not mine. However, I knew, if I was to allow God to be victorious through me, I needed to tackle this head on. As part of my healing, I knew I needed to 'emerge' from a place of strength in the Lord without carrying shame and guilt.

I recognised that I carried the guilt of not being able to hold fast to my marriage vows and therefore the vows I had made before God were broken. It was not because I had a desirable marriage that I contended the divorce. Instead, it was due to the faith given me at the time to stand against injustice along with a desire to honour the vows I'd made before the Lord. I'd wanted to remain faithful to Him in this way. But now I feared integrity in this matter was being taken from me.

I started weeping over the words I was reading

One morning, I opened my Bible to continue my reading through the book of Numbers. I was in chapter 30 when all of a sudden I started weeping over the words I was reading. My spirit was receiving something from the

Lord that my mind had not yet comprehended. His Spirit was so powerfully ministering to mine through these verses:

Now if her husband makes no response whatever to her from day to day, then he confirms all her vows or all the agreements that bind her; he confirms them, because he made no response to her on the day that he heard them. But if he does make them void after he has heard them, then he shall bear her guilt.

Numbers 30:14-15

The passage talks about a married woman's vows made to the Lord. The husband could make them void on the day he heard them, otherwise they would stand. If he made them void after that time, then he would bear the guilt of her broken vow. In that instant I knew the Lord did not hold me responsible for the divorce. My integrity and honour had not been taken from me. As my spiritual head, Michael had a responsibility to help me keep my vow to the Lord but, on the contrary, he caused the breaking of that vow and the marriage covenant, making it impossible for me to keep my promise to the Lord. Therefore, the guilt did not rest upon me. This was so releasing and a beautiful example of the living Word of God and His Spirit bringing revelation and healing to me. God freed me instantly from this guilt.

Yet I will not forget you

When the Lord showed me that divorce was permitted and that I would be heading in that direction, I wrestled with beliefs that, firstly, I was never to remarry. Secondly, should it be permissible to remarry, why would any godly man choose to take on a mother and daughter – a woman used and discarded rather than one kept pure? The Lord gave me these verses:

Can a woman forget her nursing child, and not have compassion on the son of her womb? Surely they may forget, yet I will not forget you. See, I have inscribed you on the palms of My hands; your walls are continually before Me.

Isaiah 49:15-16

The Lord had not forgotten Rebecca and me but rather He had compassion on us. The broken walls in the home were continually before Him and I knew He would rebuild them and provide for our every need. I knew the Lord delighted to take those discarded and despised, meticulously working on renewing them until they resembled a precious jewel. This, too, revealed something of His heart for Israel. It was a wonderful truth that our inheritance was in Him and His inheritance in us. I didn't have much faith that any man would view me or love me as God does. I didn't even know if I was now denied the opportunity to love another or be loved in this way. I could, however, rest in the knowledge that God is my husband and will never leave me or forsake me.

****

For Zion's sake I will not hold my peace
For Jerusalem's sake I'll not rest

Hephzibah, Beulah.
Sought out, not forsaken,
The Lord delights in you.

In His hand you'll be a crown of glory
By His mouth you'll have a new name
With His mighty hand you will reap the harvest
Through the blood of His son you have been redeemed

Watchmen on the wall shall never hold their peace
Until Jerusalem's a praise they'll give him no rest

Hephzibah, Beulah.
Sought out, not forsaken,
The Lord delights in you.

No rest until her righteousness goes forth as brightness
Salvation, as a lamp that burns.

****

LYRICS FROM 'HEPHZIBAH'
2021 SONG BY HANNAH

Did I need to pray for this gifting now?

I initially turned to YouTube in an attempt to seek sound teaching in order to better understand scriptures on divorce and remarriage. A number of questions perplexed me. Under the law of Moses, the perpetrator of adultery could suffer the death penalty, leaving the innocent party a widow (Leviticus 20:10). The widow was then free to remarry according to scripture. God's grace now extended to the adulterous offender, freeing them from the death penalty and allowing them to know His mercy and forgiveness. However, instead of the innocent party now being a widow, they may find themselves a divorcee. Did the same freedom previously allowing the innocent party to remarry still remain under the new covenant? Or did being termed a divorcee (as opposed to a widow) now mean they would be the ones carrying a life sentence of singleness and celibacy? I knew singleness and celibacy were not negative things but I was also acutely aware they were gifts and specific callings upon a person's life. Did I need to pray for this gifting now?

I knew I needed to knuckle down and study

Scanning YouTube blindly was a bad move, as it opened me up to various men and women using this platform to verbalise opinion which was not always from a place of love. Condemnation attempted to take hold of me. I knew I needed to knuckle down and study this for myself. It was very timely that I was lent a book and subsequently given literature that gave in-depth teaching and insight into the various scriptures around divorce and remarriage. One such teaching taught me the faithful translation of the scripture in Malachi 2:16, rendered by the New King James Bible as *'For the LORD God of Israel says that He hates divorce'*. A phrase I often heard to reflect this verse was 'God hates divorce'.

I was fascinated to learn more about the context of this verse; that in Malachi's time Jewish men were acting treacherously towards the Lord and their wives (they had married idol worshippers). As a result, the men hated their wives and divorced them. I was even more interested to find out that earlier transcripts like the Qumran (Dead Sea Scrolls) more faithfully translate the verse as:

'For if you have hated (and) divorced,' (says the Lord) God of Israel, 'they cover My (garment) with violence,' says the Lord of Hosts, 'so be careful in your spirit and do (not) deal treacherously.'

The words in parenthesis here represent missing words in the text. Many scholars conclude that God is not the subject of the verb 'hate' but rather the man doing the divorcing is. Other translations, like the English Standard Version, reflect this: *'For the man who does not love his wife but divorces her . . .'* The emphasis here then was not that God hates divorce but rather disapproved of the men hating their wives and divorcing them. It spoke to me of God hating the act of treacherous divorce but not hating what can be viewed as disciplinary divorce. I was at peace knowing that becoming a divorcee does not automatically mean I will be party to something God hates. This was freeing but also helped me to reconcile the Spirit's earlier leading to contend the treacherous divorce Michael had petitioned against me without valid cause. It was necessary to make a righteous stand against his motives of divorce as this had displeased the Lord.

Pastors had confessed to me that it was not a topic in which they were well versed

To my satisfaction, I found some of the revelations imparted to me by the Holy Spirit were reflected and expounded in the literature I was now reading. It was so enriching. There was so much to learn about the context in which these verses appeared in scripture, who they were spoken to, different schools of thought on divorce at the time, societal norms and the faithful translations of the Greek or Hebrew. I'd never received in-depth teaching on these matters and pastors had confessed to me that it was not a topic in which they were well versed. There was a tendency towards vagueness or skipping over certain verses when it came to divorce and remarriage but I could understand why. For my specific situation, that which I hadn't received in church, the Lord had faithfully given me by His Holy Spirit and through the vessel of the obedient evangelist. God had brought to me the verses I had needed and at the time I had needed them.

There are many misconceptions and unhelpful attitudes still broadly held

My advice for anyone finding themselves facing this issue would be to first become familiar with the Old and New Testament scriptures pertaining to divorce and remarriage, being careful to not misconstrue what they are saying and also what they aren't saying. Beyond that, when it comes to interpretation of such scriptures, there exists such a range of teachings amongst those generally considered sound Bible teachers. It can easily become overwhelming or invite the temptation to shop around until one such teaching suits our agenda or feelings. There are many misconceptions and unhelpful attitudes still broadly held on this topic which sadly imprison some behind bars of shame and guilt. Or, by contrast, other teachings convey a looseness in their approach towards the sanctity of marriage aligning more to a casual worldly attitude of something that should be held in honour.

Before embarking on this, then, I would strongly urge time is spent in prayer, asking the Holy Spirit to reveal His will through anything you will expose yourself to. Your soul may need to visit the dark but intimate place deep in the 'garden of Gethsemane' to agonisingly accomplish a surrendering to God's will over your own, knowing His will is always better for you. Ensuring your heart and motives are pure and ready to receive whatever the Holy Spirit desires to impart on this matter of marriage, divorce and remarriage, is essential. In some areas, it may be that conviction and repentance is required, and in others, there may be a release from guilt and shame. We can be confident that the Holy Spirit will deal sensitively and faithfully with us unto our freedom and spiritual growth. Therefore, to invite Him into this process is paramount.

Diligently study and come to your own convictions and conclusions by the leading of God's Holy Spirit

I would love to share further insight from my studies on this matter but I fear I would be straying from the directive the Lord has given me for this book, namely to testify of His mighty deliverance. It is also not my place, and there lies a danger: to indirectly imply through my own conclusions that another is in sin or, equally damaging, endorse any action that may well be sinful. Where guidance is needed, I trust the Lord has placed you under spiritual authorities that can diligently and prayerfully judge your unique situation in light of scripture. However, I will reference some literature resources at the end of this story for those who admiringly desire to be 'Bereans' on this subject matter. I have made sure to include materials that offer different arguments and interpretations that you may diligently study and come to your own convictions and conclusions by the leading of God's Holy Spirit. What each reference does agree on and assure us of, however, is that marriage is designed by God, it is sacred and to be honoured. The sanctity of marriage must be held in supremacy.

For now we see in a mirror, dimly,
but then face to face. Now I know in part,
but then I shall know just as I also am known.

1 Corinthians 13:12

Some Reflections

I hope by now you have gleaned that I am just a normal, imperfect woman who had a story to tell of a perfect God's touch upon her life. I cannot share the following reflections from any great height. On the contrary, the lessons I learned had to be received in a lowly place. Fully aware of my own weaknesses, I depend on the Lord each and every day.

Having been given the directive to write this book, I was then dependent on the Lord's enabling and provision to fulfil this, trusting His hand would be upon it. I know God will provide the finances for its production and that He will ensure it is placed in the hands of those most needing to receive it. Indeed, if you are reading this, you too now know God met this need and all glory goes to Him. Already, He has graciously shown me His touch upon this book. Until I counted through the songs quoted in this book, I had no idea there were twelve. Biblically, this is a number that often represents completeness, God's authority and power, and the coming of His kingdom. God knew. I had no idea the number of chapters I would write would be forty, the number used for wilderness days, trials and testing. God knew.

I know the trials, tribulations and pain you have faced won't necessarily be the same as mine. However, I hope I can point you to Jesus who has already walked through them all, and to the Holy Spirit, who is present in them all. And, of course, to the Father, who oversees them all for He is the God who sees. He saw Hagar and her son in their desperation in the wilderness and He sees my daughter and me. He sees you too. Perhaps the following pages will allow you also to see a glimpse of God.

Content in all weathers

Learning to be content in all situations is an ongoing process as the Lord exposes us to a variety of different climates throughout our lifetimes. As soon as we adapt to one particular climate, the next weather system moves in and the process begins again. It is necessary for moulding our characters and developing our dependency on Him.

Already in my life I had been exposed to a number of challenging weather fronts. I'd known the feeling of abandonment that comes with desertion, the belittling and betrayal with abuse, and the pain and reproach of facing divorce. Having mourned over 'losing' my husband and separating from him, I had in part tasted widowhood. I knew all too well the sharp stabs of loneliness in singleness as well as its more subtle shadow that can lurk within marriage. I'd been uprooted from familiar places and people, and spent time behind prison bars of control, unhelpful 'labels' and my own religiosity. I was familiar with the struggles of being a single mother – being acutely aware of what it is to both have money and not to have enough. I had walked through the deep sorrow of losing a baby and then the releasing of my other daughter, here on earth, out of my full-time care into someone else's hands. I'd faced rejection and hurt within the body of Christ and endured misunderstanding, judgement and a harshness from those I loved.

Did I resent the violent storms, oppressive clouds, biting frost, unrelenting downpours, insufferable heat, bitter winds, disorientating fog or eerie mist which I had journeyed through? The honest answer would be, at times, whilst in the midst of them, yes. But now, the very idea of basking in a continual, comfortable sunshine had lost its allure. The weathers of affliction had invigorated and revived me. I felt alive. How could I now recline into dozing under a sunshine of ignorance and apathy? Other than producing an outward tan with its superficial glow, it was destined to wane and would fail to produce the inward character so needed to walk this hard and narrow path with Christ. I wanted *'the genuineness of [my] faith, being much more precious than gold that perishes, though it is tested by fire . . . to praise, honour, and glory at the revelation of Jesus Christ'* (1 Peter 1:7).

You have dealt well with Your servant, O LORD, according to Your word. Teach me good judgement and knowledge, for I believe Your commandments. Before I was afflicted I went astray, but now I keep Your word. You are good, and do good; teach me Your statutes. The proud have forged a lie against me, but I will keep Your precepts with my whole heart. Their heart is as fat as grease, but I delight in Your law. It is good for me that I have been afflicted, that I may learn Your statutes. The law of Your mouth is better to me than thousands of coins of gold and silver.

Psalm 119:65-72

Within my marriage, I had to accept the circumstances I found myself in by allowing any bitterness to be turned into something sweet. (Accepting the circumstances doesn't of course justify or condone them.) Instead of trying to flee that which was out of my control, I was to instead acclimatise. Whether it be holding up an umbrella of grace and forgiveness, clothing myself in the waterproofs that guard, or embracing the companion sent to bear the brunt with me, God provided what I needed. It was my choice to ensure no bitterness would take root but it was the touch of Jesus that accomplished the transformational work in my heart. He led me to pools of bitter disappointments, as He did the Israelites, to test whether I would respond in faith and prayer or by grumbling and complaining. By applying the cross of Calvary and choosing faith and prayer, the bitter waters of Marah could be healed and sweetened. The Lord brought me to a place where I knew such love and blessing through His death on the cross for me. This meant I could release what I had received towards Michael, freely loving him irrespective of His behaviour towards me. I accepted my circumstances may never change and committed to remaining in the marriage. I soon realised even under the burden and yoke that was weighing down upon me, God's grace was enough. It wasn't until I had learned to say, *'Whatever my lot, it is well with my soul,'* that God orchestrated my deliverance. Until I could overcome bitterness at Marah, I wasn't fit to endure the remainder of the wilderness journey.

Consider it pure joy, my brothers and sisters, whenever you face trials of many kinds, because you know that the testing of your faith produces perseverance. Let perseverance finish its work so that you may be mature and complete, not lacking anything.

James 1:2-4 (NIV)

****

When grumblings are arising,
In me
And I find myself despising,
What I see

Focusing on all that's wrong
In life
In my own strength carrying on
With strife

I'll draw near to You
You draw near to me
I'll draw to You
You draw near to me

You turn my bitter water sweet
Your Word, a lamp unto my feet
You give me grace again and again
I'll do it all unto You, my Lord
Not men.

When myself I can't look past
Blinded
God's provision I have not asked
Misguided

When resentment has been exposed
In me
In filthy garments I am clothed
Dirty.

So I'll lift my eyes
Where does my help come from?
So I'll lift my eyes
Where does my help come from?

Who am I that You should be at all mindful of me?
Faithful One, just and true
Change me to be more like You
More of You, less of me
O what precious mercy
Lamb of God, King of Kings
Cover me under Your mighty wings

My cup, it overflows, thank You Jesus

****

LYRICS FROM 'SWEET WATER'
2020 SONG BY HANNAH

Freedom

So often I would wrestle over my circumstances in prayer, wanting God to change them and give me victory over them. Yet along my journey I continued to taste the bitter pools of disappointment and apparent defeats. 'Winning' should never have been the ultimate goal. Instead, the revelations of God's character through the trials and my refinement to become more like Him were where the precious and eternal treasures lay. His work, underground, to establish deeper roots was the key to a healthy and strong tree above ground.

Marriage is to be honoured and defended, worked at and fought for. It is also not to be idolised and neither is our spouse or our children. Marriage is a gift from God and if we abuse that gift and do not use it to glorify and reflect Him, in His sovereignty, He has every right to allow the removal of that gift. God taught me, when necessary, He will send that fire of division in order to fulfil a greater purpose – He desires a purified and radiant bride. He so longs for her and is jealous for her. Thus, our longing above all else should be for Him. My earthly marriage, instead of being a reflection of the devotion between Christ and His church, had climaxed into a grave portrayal of something very different. It had become a bondage prohibiting my very expression of devotion towards Jesus. I was Jesus' betrothed, yet I was under the bondage of Pharaoh in Egypt, restricted in bringing Him my sacrifice. Jesus fought for me and my release. Time and messages were given to Pharaoh to allow repentance but he refused to soften his heart. In the end, just as it was with Pharaoh, it appeared that God had hardened Michael's heart, and made a miraculous way of escape where there appeared to be none. He delivered me to a wilderness. Why? *'That you may know that there is none like Me [God] in all the earth'* (Exodus 9:14).

Freedom comes at a cost. Our sin cost Jesus His life to set us free and it'll cost us something to walk in that freedom if we are to overcome our sinful flesh, this poisonous world and the father of lies. I realised that freedom from bondage comes by yielding to and recognising the Holy Spirit as our power, Jesus as our answer and the Father as the director of our steps.

God has not given us a spirit of fear but of power, of love and of sound mind

I had worked with domestic abuse victims and vulnerable people for over ten years and attended many child protection, police and social services meetings. If this experience was anything to go by, I knew that naturally and statistically speaking I 'should' have mental health problems, and Rebecca behavioural issues, as a bare minimum. All too familiar now was this diagnosis of 'anxiety and depression' in nearly all those who approached me at work, having had similar traumas to mine. Their 'treatment' would often comprise of a concoction of medications prescribed by doctors; as their anxiety and depression increased so did their dosage. Without minimising the reality of these conditions and how quality of life can be affected as a result, it both saddened and frustrated me that this was now becoming the accepted norm and culture of today.

It has become common practice both in the world and in the church to accept living with mental illness as someone's lot in life. Where are the voices saying we can *live without* these labels and medication? Was it because I am strong that I escaped ongoing anxiety, depression and post-traumatic stress disorder? Is Rebecca a special child that she remained unscathed? No. I am no stronger than any other woman and Rebecca no more favoured than the next child. It is God alone who preserved, delivered and healed us. He promises a sound mind but it involved my cooperation. I was given no special immunity against depression, anxiety, worry, fear, self-pity, enemy lies, suicidal thoughts and anger, which I had, at times, crouching at my door. They are not to be tolerated. The enemy would love nothing more than for us to let these entities in to reside with us to obstruct our effectiveness for the Lord. I was living proof that those who have lived through similar traumas to mine could be wholly preserved by the Lord and His Word alone.

When you pass through the waters, I will be with you; and through the rivers, they shall not overflow you. When you walk through the fire, you shall not be burned, nor shall the flame scorch you.

Isaiah 43:2

The key for me in overcoming my own issues was to take my focus from myself and lift my eyes to the Lord; the Alpha and Omega, the worker of miracles. Having studied psychology at university, I could see its strong influence in today's society. I was mindful that it was restrictive in as much as it was only man's study of man and not God's insight of man. How much better it is to esteem our Creator's perspective of man as revealed by His Word! When the practice of psychology teaches the study of man in light of God's Word, it then has something of value to offer. Regarding man, we discover within the Bible two opposing truths that exist in perfect harmony. The first: *'All have sinned and fall short of the glory of God'* (Romans 3:23). The second: we have a wholesome and complete worthiness in Christ. Meditation on the second, especially for domestic abuse victims when exposure to degrading remarks and emotional abuse has occurred, is especially important. Therefore, having determined man's unmerited favour through Jesus' sacrifice at Calvary we continue in our journey to discover more of God's character through His Word. The more we see God, the less we see of ourselves, allowing our perspective to be transformed and our faith to flourish.

Unto You I lift up my eyes, O You who dwell in the heavens. Behold, as the eyes of servants look to the hand of their masters, as the eyes of a maid to the hand of her mistress, so our eyes look to the LORD our God, until He has mercy on us.

Psalm 123:1-2

Sabbath is made for man, not man for the Sabbath

I was desperate to be freed from affliction and the circumstances that oppressed and crippled me. In moments of desperation I cried out to God many times over the thirteen-year marriage. God was more than able to take the cup of suffering from me and I knew that. However, at that time, He required me to continue further. My will in those difficult moments was not His will. The conflict between our will and the Lord's is a very real and agonising struggle. It is not because He doesn't love us that we are sometimes required to further endure suffering. It is because

He does love us. He has more to work into us, more to work out of us and greater purposes than we will understand at the time. Unlike Jesus, we will not have to endure every suffering He had to: *'God is faithful, who will not allow you to be tempted beyond what you are able, but with the temptation will also make the way of escape, that you may be able to bear it'* (1 Corinthians 10:13).

There are a number of examples in the gospel stories of those who were desperate for Jesus to deliver and heal them. The gospel writers allow us in, in part to see and hear these scenes of healing and deliverance as they occurred at their appointed times. Yet, never far away from the miracle was the Pharisee. Jesus' method and way of working very often offended their beliefs and the law they held so tightly onto. Sadly, this resulted in a focus on perceived failings and error, blinding them from seeing the fruit. I, too, held a religiosity about not becoming divorced. Had I not surrendered to the fact divorce could be God's way of freeing me, I would have robbed myself of the freedom, hope and future being offered to me. God calls us to peace and not bondage. *'The letter kills, but the Spirit gives life'* (2 Corinthians 3:6).

I had to conclude that anyone who could not get past the impending divorce to see the miraculous deliverance and preservation of Rebecca and me, failed to see something of the heart of God. We should not try to put God into a box which fits our own pre-conceived ideas. Instead, we must expand our understanding to appreciate God's ways simply cannot be contained. They are instead to shape us. New wine cannot be poured into old wine skins (Mark 2:22). It will burst the vessel and leave us with nothing. When new wine (alive and fermenting) is poured into a new wine skin, the wine skin stretches and reshapes in accordance to the expansion of the wine. I had to accept God's higher ways by faith and allow some essential reshaping of my pre-established beliefs around divorce.

The preferred narrative would have been for my husband to be freed from his bondage and transformed, with the marriage restored. However, it seemed I was required to walk a different path. Yet, had I experienced a restoration of my marriage without walking the painful and traumatic journey towards divorce, what would have been my heart for divorcees, single parents and children in broken homes who permeate our world today? Would I have cared for them, known God's heart for them and been able to minister to them with the same love and compassion? Probably not. Although I'd been unable to touch and rescue one man due to the hardening of his heart and the powers of darkness, God could use what was meant for evil to save many more:

But as for you, you meant evil against me; but God meant it for good, in order to bring it about as it is this day, to save many people alive.

Genesis 50:20

Wisdom for women

I had observed two responses amongst women dissatisfied in a marriage where abuse or contentions may be apparent. I have termed them as 'fight' or 'flight' responses as I have no doubt they are adopted as a means of survival. Whom we 'fight' and to where we take 'flight' make all the difference in whether these responses lead to a woman overcoming or, instead, into the snares of the enemy and further bondage.

Women can be mistaken in thinking that they must 'fight' an oppressive spouse. After all, is not society's paradigm of the 'strong, feminist woman' to stand up for oneself, stand your ground and give as good as you get to any man that acts the bully? Attempting to control, manipulate and overpower a man, it seems in today's world, is perfectly justifiable in such circumstances. Surely, where hurt and betrayal have been experienced, a toughening up must take place? If a woman is to survive further breaking of the heart she must attempt to build her defensive wall around it that no man may gain entry again. I would oppose this view. I am not suggesting there is no 'fight' to be had. Rather, the wrestle is not against flesh and blood but against powers and principalities – those things pertaining to the enemy (Ephesians 6:12). It is in the place of the prayer closet where anger can be unleashed, the voice can be raised, undignified sobbing is allowed and a frank petitioning of the Lord can take place. It is in the refuge of the prayer closet, a woman must allow God right into the centre of the pain she is experiencing, knowing He is near to the broken-hearted and saves those crushed in spirit (Psalm 34:18).

There is a godly strength to be seen, not in the fighting or overbearing of a man, but in good character. My conduct and behaviour as a wife was not dependent on who my husband was. I was not responsible for my husband's behaviour, but I was responsible for my own. I was also not to listen to his account of who I was but receive God's truth on who I was, *'for in Him we live and move and have our being'* (Acts 17:28). By studying examples of obedient women in scripture, we can trace the beautiful undertones of their godly strength. Their strength did not seek to oppose men nor challenge their God-given authority. However, the influence these women had was undeniable. The loyal and virtuous character of Ruth, courage and grace of Esther, dedication and insight of Anna, intercession and tenacity of Deborah, wisdom and boldness of Abigail, shrewdness and resilience of Tamar, devotion and submission of Mary and faithfulness and persistence of Hannah all have much to teach us. There are many more examples I could mention. Each woman had their appointed time to arise, show their strength of character and bring glory to God.

The Bible tells us how wives are to respect, submit to and obey their husbands as unto the Lord (Ephesians 5:22 and 1 Peter 3:1). Husbands are also instructed to love their wives as Christ loved the church (Ephesians 5:25). So how does this look for women in relationships where the wife is not loved or cherished? No different. It was paramount that I remain a godly example to Michael in our marriage so that perhaps he may be won over by my conduct. In my case, this was not the outcome (at least not yet) but with the Lord nothing is wasted. My offering was unto the Lord, and our daughter had seen this example. Had I not sought to behave as blamelessly as possible, I have no doubt I would have been describing incidents far worse than the ones detailed in this book. I failed at times and stumbled but, by God's mercy, was not utterly cast down for the Lord upheld me (Psalm 37:24). That said, witnessing from within the home may not always remain the right decision. God values preservation of life and where there is serious risk of harm (physical or emotional) posed for a woman or their children, taking refuge and separation must remain an option. This is not an unbiblical concept.

It is important to seek the Lord for each scenario and, where possible, seek godly council. Seeking godly council may feel disloyal and uncomfortable. Naturally, out of respect for our spouse, to protect privacy or out of fear, we favour discretion in the sharing of marital problems. The caution in the disclosure of personal details within a marriage is right and proper for most marriages. However, it is not wrong, and is in fact wise, to disclose to a trusted friend or godly authority when the behaviour of a spouse reaches a point where prayer, support and outside intervention is needed.

Obeying the Lord may at times mean disobeying an ungodly husband and therefore the consequences of this may place you temporarily at greater risk. However, I learned that yielding to anything other than God led to further bondage, and where a stand was needed according to God's will, He protected me and made a way to obey Him. There is no safer place than in the will of God. 'Fighting' by holding onto faith and the Word of God is so essential. I am confident that for those who do this and face similar battles to mine, you will see one of the following three outcomes: a break-through in the situation, a deliverance out of the situation, or further grace given to endure through the situation. It may seem, at times, abiding in the wisdom of God bears no fruit and is hopelessly unproductive. Do not lose heart, for the Lord is working in the unseen (behind the scenes) when nothing is visible to the natural eye. His timing is perfect and He will fight for you.

We have seen how to 'fight' and how not to 'fight' as a response in difficult marital situations. The other response I have observed is 'flight'. It is here that we see a more subtle and deceptive snare set for women as it involves a deception from her own heart. Proverbs 4:23 tells us to keep our hearts with all diligence, for out of them spring the issues of life. Dissatisfaction and loneliness within marriage and outside of marriage can invite the temptation to take flight and escape these hardships. The widespread issue of pornography, which traps many men, is tackled on some levels within the church but there is very little exposure of the damage that ideologies presented in modern romance films and novels can have for the woman. Some stories may even pass themselves off as being 'Christian romance' but such branding is usually deceptive. From a young age, many girls are exposed to seemingly innocent films that infuse the false ideologies of a 'flawless prince' and ending with a marriage ceremony. The impermanence of romance means it is never good to encourage this as the test or standard for selecting a husband. Such philosophies imply romance as the foundational factor for a happy and lasting relationship without looking beyond to character and virtue. Repeated exposure to such material can create a false reality in a woman's thoughts and place an unrealistic standard upon a man. These things will never fulfil the lack that first caused the indulgence but, instead, can invite a sensuality and lust; that is to reach out after something with the purpose of appropriating it. Idolising another man or marriage (whether one in existence or one in something we read or watch), is sinful and will lead to bondage. No matter how neglected a woman may feel, taking flight into unhealthy fantastical imaginations can lead to sinful outcomes. For the single woman there is a danger love will be awakened before its time (Song of Solomon 8:4) and for the married woman, it may result in betrayal towards her husband.

In both cases it can cause damage and issues in relationships (whether current or future ones). Instead, an acknowledgement and identification from where this destructive seed has begun its germination is essential. This must be followed by an intentional and complete uprooting and severing from the offensive source. Failure to uproot will undoubtedly cause the seed to produce bad fruit. All thoughts should be brought into captivity (2 Corinthians 10:5) with meditation being upon that which is pure, lovely and good (Philippians 4:8).

However, I don't just want to apply platitudes to situations that I know to contain deep and complex emotional struggles involving rejection and unreciprocated love. Leah in the Bible knew what it was to be unloved by her husband. She wrestled through to a place of praise of the Lord, reflecting this in the name given to her fourth son, 'Judah', meaning 'praise'. The Lord had greater purposes for Leah that went beyond her immediate rejection. Our Lord Himself was crucified by the very people He came for and gave His life for. He still yearns for the love of His people, the Jews. God knows your pain, and you are in a privileged position, that many others won't be in, to feel something of the pain in His heart. This is precious and an opportunity for you to allow your pain to knit you ever closer to your Lord. *'Weeping may endure for a night, but joy comes in the morning'* (Psalm 30:5) and there is a hope and a greater purpose awaiting you.

There is a pure and safe person to take flight to. He is your refuge and holds a beauty to be embraced, more lovely than anything obtained through our own strength or visited within our own imagination. I was blessed in that the Holy Spirit enlightened the eyes of my understanding to the best romantic narrative interwoven throughout the books of scripture. This romance has *agápē* love at its core. The Bible starts with an earthly marriage (as does this book) but finishes with our marriage to Christ. This is where God directed my focus and affections. Matthew 6:33 tells us to *'seek first the kingdom of God and His righteousness, and all these things shall be added to you'*. As the bride of Christ, we have a perfect husband and marriage to come. He is continually wooing and seeking out a cleansed and virtuous bride for Himself. Christ, who gave His life for us and is the fairest and most beautiful among ten thousand, desires us. Surely any dissatisfaction on earth dissipates as we fix our eyes on our beloved. A fulfilling union can be known with Him on earth with the promise we will one day see him face to face (1 Corinthians 13:12) and be with Him for the rest of eternity.

****

Let me tell about someone I'm getting to know
He started wooing me many years ago
He called patiently until His voice I heard
At His touch this dead heart slowly stirred

Let me tell you how this someone rescued me
I was stumbling in the darkness and couldn't see
He opened up my eyes, I saw all my sin
He took all my shame, let His light flood in

Coming back to my first love again

My beloved is mine and I am His
I am my beloved's, He is mine
I am my beloved's and His desire is toward me

Let me tell you more about the one I'm getting to know
His love the waters cannot quench, nor overflow
His faithfulness and steadfast love extend to the skies
He leads me perfectly for He is mighty and wise

Coming back to my first love again

****

Lyrics from 'His Desire is Toward Me'
2021 Song by Hannah

182

Love your enemies

But I say to you, love your enemies, bless those who curse you, do good to those who hate you, and pray for those who spitefully use you and persecute you.

Matthew 5:44

It is easy to carry about us an air of loving all whilst flippantly turning the other cheek to those we feel hard done by. We like to do this in full view of people from whom we desire to reap praise. Perhaps we can liken it to spraying the skin with perfume – providing that immediate and pleasing fragrance, appreciated by those in close proximity. However, it is not until we are hard pressed that it can truly be known what kind of fragrance will be emitted from beneath the skin. God will set us in those wilderness and valley environments, out of sight of others, to test what is in our hearts. I do not know what it truly is to be persecuted for the sake of Christ (in the way we may view persecution of Christians) and I think I am safe in assuming most in the West don't either. I do know that the persecuted church prays for us; they see many more miracles and know Christ in a way we cannot because of enduring persecution. It was one thing for me to make a stand in public, receiving an onslaught of abuse for righteousness' sake during pro-life displays. In these moments, the abuse was likely momentary and the abuser I would probably never see again. However, my real testing came from behind closed doors – the test of enduring rejection and suffering from the very man I had given myself to and loved, believing he would love me, protect me and provide for me. Instead, I found myself bound in captivity and easily accessible for the enemy to persecute me. I had to learn to bless Michael when he cursed me and love him when he was unfaithful and harsh towards me. These are the wilderness sacrifices God is looking for from His bride – not the loveless noise of a clanging symbol. Are we willing to suffer the wounds that are necessary to harvest the precious frankincense and myrrh in our lives? Without such we cannot expect to produce their pleasing aroma for the Lord.

The days we are living in are becoming increasingly dark. Evil is called good and good called evil (Isaiah 5:20). It won't be long before the marginalisation and persecution of faithful Christians here rapidly increases. It was a sobering realisation knowing all I had endured and given up to follow Christ was merely preparation and training for what is inevitably coming. It is only through knowing Christ and His refining work in us that we will be able to endure further onslaught from Satan. If we cannot ooze that *agápē* love for one another within the church, and extend it to those who wrong us now, how will we fair when real persecution hits our land? No longer will superficial sacrifices suffice. The bride of Christ needs to prepare to offer her beloved a more costly sacrifice as she enters the wilderness.

****

Freed from a captive land
He'll lead her by the hand, to stand
Alone, in the wilderness

Then He'll search far and wide
For hearts tested and tried, a bride
Loyal, through the wilderness

**Arise, bride, and bring
Your sacrifice to Him
Prepare, bride, to bring
The purest offering
In the wilderness, in the wilderness**

**Do not give to your beloved,
Nor offer to the King
That which cost you nothing**

When in the desert land,
He'll help with His right hand, her stand
Up strong, in this wilderness

She'll grasp love deep and wide
Her heart now meek and tried, a bride,
Loyal, through the wilderness

She'll come out leaning on Him.

****

LYRICS FROM 'LOYAL THROUGH THE WILDERNESS'

2023 SONG BY HANNAH

*When a man's ways please the L*ORD*,*
he makes even his enemies to be at peace with him.

Proverbs 16:7

40.

Up From The Wilderness, Leaning On Her Beloved

He asked for my prayers

The Israelites endured forty years in the wilderness. My wilderness journey lasted four years. The story didn't end free from a final twist. It was one that had potential to change the whole course of events and challenged me again regarding the route God was mapping out before me.

One morning in October 2023, I received a message from Michael, admitting his helpless state and his need for God. Regretful and remorseful and in reference to the divorce, he posed the question, *'It's not too late for me to put an end to it all, is it?'* He was experiencing some guilt from his actions against me and the Lord and this had taken its toll on his mental state, causing him some vexation. I do not know what triggered this and did not ask. He asked for my prayers and halted following through with the final part of the divorce. I reiterated my forgiveness towards him. For the first time in a long while, Michael was seemingly at peace with me.

I knew only that I was to lay this contact from him before the Lord

Was this God working a genuine repentance in him or had the enemy thrown in a deceptive curve ball just before the conclusion of the divorce? Did more time and grace need to be given that there might be a softening of his heart? Would he go through with the divorce and release me or was the guilt of divorcing me 'treacherously' now too much for his conscience?

Would I have to be the one to finalise the divorce on what some may consider are biblical disciplinary grounds of adultery, desertion and abuse to relieve his troubled conscience? Or was God restoring Michael unto himself and preserving our marriage?

By now, four years on from where this testimony began, his contact and the questions it posed stirred no emotional response from me. Of course I was pained that Michael was experiencing some kind of mental torment. With boundaries in place and from a distance, I fed to him the Word of God as I would have to anyone else experiencing this. I knew only that I was to lay this contact from him before the Lord and await His answer. Sure enough, His answer came.

'Team restore' or 'team rescue'

No doubt you've already decided if you are on 'team restore' or 'team rescue' in this narrative and await to know if God restored Michael to Himself, preserving the marriage, or whether He instead rescued me from the enemy and permitted divorce? I'm not to tell you. Like Moses, you can only be taken through the journey and not into the destination, as, in this instance, the destination is not to supersede or steal from the testimony of the journey. What I can tell you is that the Lord inspired me to write this book as a married woman lest some may be impeded in their reading because of their views on divorce. The Lord does not want my status to hinder any in receiving the lessons the Holy Spirit desires to impart. I am not to set a precedent that every marriage can be saved or that divorce is always the way of deliverance. Anyone facing a similar scenario must allow God alone to write their story.

Be cautioned, though. If Numbers 33 is anything to go by (the chapter God used to instruct me to write this book), embarking on a wilderness journey will not be free from:

- sets backs and becoming trapped at Migdol before a miraculous escape (Numbers 33:7-8),
- overcoming bitterness at Marah (Numbers 33:8),

- restoration and refreshment at Elim (Numbers 33:9),
- need of provision and a battle at Rephidim (Numbers 33:14),
- intercession and obedience to God's commands at Sinai (Numbers 33:15),
- overcoming grumbling and temptation to return at Kibroth Hattaavah (Numbers 33:16),
- judgement from others at Hazeroth (Numbers 33:17),
- death at Mount Hor (Numbers 33:38).

What still lay ahead

And what about the calling to Leigh Park, whether serving there as a married woman or a single mother? To answer, let us stick with Numbers 33. I've responded to the command to write down the journey (verses 1-2), the journey has been testified of (verses 3-49) and so now we arrive at verses 50-56; and our clue as to what still lay ahead:

Now the LORD spoke to Moses in the plains of Moab by the Jordan, across from Jericho, saying, 'Speak to the children of Israel, and say to them: "When you have crossed the Jordan into the land of Canaan, then you shall drive out all the inhabitants of the land from before you, destroy all their engraved stones, destroy all their moulded images, and demolish all their high places; you shall dispossess the inhabitants of the land and dwell in it, for I have given you the land to possess. And you shall divide the land by lot as an inheritance among your families; to the larger you shall give a larger inheritance, and to the smaller you shall give a smaller inheritance; there everyone's inheritance shall be whatever falls to him by lot. You shall inherit according to the tribes of your fathers. But if you do not drive out the inhabitants of the land from before you, then it shall be that those whom you let remain shall be irritants in your eyes and thorns in your sides, and they shall harass you in the land where you dwell. Moreover it shall be that I will do to you as I thought to do to them."'

Numbers 33:50-56

The conquest for the land of Leigh Park was still to come, which no doubt one day would be a testimony worthy of its own book. There were strongholds to be broken – if we did not rise up, fight and intercede, the enemy would extend his reach and our children and future generations would suffer. I now understood one reason Moses was instructed to write down the wilderness journey in Numbers 33. Recalling the faithfulness of God through a wilderness journey was essential for instilling the faith needed for the conquest ahead. I now press on in full assurance of God's complete faithfulness, knowing all He purposes will be accomplished. I can confidently say with David:

*'If it had not been the LORD who was on our side,' let Israel now say – 'If it had not been the LORD who was on our side, when men rose up against us, then they would have swallowed us alive, when their wrath was kindled against us; then the waters would have overwhelmed us, the stream would have gone over our soul; then the swollen waters would have gone over our soul.' Blessed be the LORD, who has not given us as prey to their teeth. Our soul has **escaped as a bird from the snare** of the fowlers; the snare is broken, and we have escaped. Our help is in the name of the LORD, who made heaven and earth.*

Psalm 124

Abortion Statistics

- Over 820 abortions are carried out every working day in the UK.
- 1 in 3 women will have an abortion before the age of 45.
- 42.4% of women who had an abortion last year, had one or more previous abortions.
- 99% of abortions are funded by the NHS.
- 97% of abortions are performed on healthy mothers and healthy babies and where sexual intercourse has been consented to.
- Around 1% of abortions are due to rape.
- Gender, eye colour and other traits are determined at conception, also known as fertilisation. At fertilisation, a new and unique human being comes into existence with its own distinct genetic code.
- Between January and June 2022, 123,219 babies, whose mothers resided in England and Wales, were killed by abortion. This compares with 105,488 over the same period in 2021, and thus represents an increase of 16.8% or 17,731 additional abortions.
- In the first half of the year, 67% of abortions in England and Wales were performed up to and including 7 weeks gestation; with 93% being performed up to and including 12 weeks.
- A recent study estimated that around 73 million babies are killed globally by abortion each year.
- **Full or partial home abortions are now the most common procedures, accounting for 82.7% of all abortions in Scotland in 2022.**

(www.cbruk.org/facts)

Domestic Abuse Statistics

- The police recorded 1,500,369 domestic abuse-related incidents and crimes in England and Wales in the year ending March 2022. The number of domestic abuse-related crimes increased 7.7% compared to the previous year.

- A domestic abuse-related call is made to the police every 30 seconds.

- The risk of serious assault and death is highest for a woman after she leaves an abusive relationship. According to the Femicide Census, 38% of women killed by their ex-partner from 2009 to 2018 were killed within the first month of separation and 89% in the first year.

- Women are more likely to be victims of high-risk or severe domestic abuse: 95% of those going to MARAC or accessing an IDVA service are women. But men are also at risk of serious assault and death from their partners.

- Seven women a month are killed by a current or former partner in England and Wales.

- 130,000 children live in homes where there is high-risk domestic abuse.

- 62% of children living with domestic abuse are directly harmed by the perpetrator of the abuse, in addition to the harm caused by witnessing the abuse of others.

- On average victims at high risk of serious harm or murder live with domestic abuse for 2-3 years before getting help.

- 85% of victims sought help on average five times from professionals in the year before they got effective help to stop the abuse.

- On average victims experience 50 incidents of abuse before getting effective help.

- Each year there are over 1 million calls to police in England and Wales about domestic abuse, and on average someone contacts the police every 30 seconds for help with domestic abuse.

- 78% of high-risk victims report the abuse to the police in the year before they get effective help, on average 2.8 times each.

- 68% of high-risk victims try to leave in the year before getting effective help, on average 2 or 3 times each.

- 23% of high-risk victims attend A&E as a result of their injuries in the year before getting effective help, many multiple times.

- A third (34%) of children in high-risk domestic abuse households are not known to children's social care.

- At least 80% of children in domestic abuse households are known to at least one public agency.

- There are 270,000 crimes reported each year related to domestic abuse in England and Wales.

- There are 6,400 domestic abuse-related sexual offences, 96,000 domestic abuse-related assaults with injury and 27,300 domestic abuse-related harassment crimes recorded by police each year in England and Wales.

- Domestic abuse-related crime forms 8% of total crime, and 11% of all sexual offences, 33% of all recorded assaults with injury, and 49% of all recorded harassment crimes in England and Wales.

- In 2013-14 there were 78,000 prosecutions for domestic abuse offences. The conviction rate for domestic violence offences in England and Wales was 75%.

- 64% of all harassment and stalking prosecutions and 77% of all restraining order breaches in England and Wales in 2013-14 were domestic violence related.

(https://safelives.org.uk/policy-evidence/about-domestic-abuse)

Divorce Statistics

- In England and Wales, the Divorce, Dissolution and Separation Act 2020 allows 'no-fault' divorce. Previously the five basic grounds for divorce were:

  1. Adultery
  2. Unreasonable behaviour
  3. Desertion
  4. The parties to the marriage have lived apart for at least two years and both consent to the divorce
  5. The parties have lived apart for at least five years.

- In 2019, there were 117,723 divorces in the UK. The percentage of married couples who divorce each year remains under 1% in England and Wales.

- An estimated 42% of marriages in England and Wales end in divorce. The most recent figures available show that almost half (45%) of divorces in England and Wales involved children aged under 16 living in the family.

- The divorce rate in England and Wales fell from a peak of 14.2 per thousand married population in 1993 to 8.4 in 2020. This is partly due to the growth of cohabitation and correspondingly fewer people getting married – the percentage of the eligible population that was married in 2002 was around 55%, and this had fallen to approximately 50% by 2020. Those who do get married are more likely to believe in the importance of it and be committed to it.

- Estimates from 2021 show that just over a fifth (22%) of dependent children in the UK live in lone-parent families (which includes divorced, separated or widowed). It still needs to be remembered that around 64% of children live in a family headed by a heterosexual married couple.

- In 1936 there were some 5,788 divorces. Then came the more liberal provisions of the 1937 Matrimonial Causes Act: in 1939 there were 9,144 divorces.

- By 1961 there were around 27,000 divorces. In 1972 (the year after the 1969 Divorce Reform Act came into force) the number was around 125,000.
- For those married in 1968 in England and Wales, 20% of marriages had ended in divorce by their 15th wedding anniversary. For those married in 2005, 29% of marriages had ended by this time.
- There are sincerely held differences of view amongst creedally orthodox churches on the question of remarriage after divorce. There are essentially two views. Some do not allow remarriage at all; others permit it only for the innocent spouse.
- Amongst Protestants, theological conservatives can be found in both groups.
- The Church of England teaches that marriage is for life. Its longstanding position until relatively recently was to permit divorce but not remarriage since it was argued that in God's sight the couple were still married. However, in 2002 the House of Bishops issued a guidance document to clergy stating that in exceptional circumstances, a divorced person may marry again in church during the lifetime of a former spouse. The Church of England's canon law remains unchanged.
- The Roman Catholic Church believes divorce is immoral and a grave offence against the natural law. It therefore considers remarriage while both husband and wife are alive as adultery. The Roman Catholic Church has said: 'It can happen that when one of the spouses is the innocent victim of a divorce decreed by civil law; this spouse therefore has not contravened the moral law. There is a considerable difference between a spouse who has sincerely tried to be faithful to the sacrament of marriage and is unjustly abandoned, and one who through his own grave fault destroys a canonically valid marriage.'
- The Westminster Confession (1647) associated with Presbyterian churches permits divorce and remarriage for the innocent party in the case of adultery.
- Historically, for centuries the tendency was for churches of all

denominations not to permit any divorce at all. They only allowed legal separation (i.e. non-cohabitation) of spouses and even then only where one spouse had committed a serious sin against the other, such as adultery. Both parties remained legally married and therefore could not remarry.

- Outside the UK the reformers permitted remarriage after divorce for the innocent party. But despite the theoretical possibility of divorce and remarriage, after a detailed study of court records in Reformation Germany, Joel Harrington found that divorce was 'a relatively little exercised option'. The possibility of collusion in order to obtain a divorce 'was considered so great by Protestant authorities that they would not even consider allowing remarriage unless the innocent spouse was free of any suspicion and willing to endure a series of legal and financial obstacles intended to dissuade him or her from such a course'.

- A 2018 estimate placed the total cost of family breakdown to the UK at over £51 billion a year.

- A child of separated parents has a higher probability of:

  - Performing less well in school;
  - Being homeless;
  - Being in trouble with the police;
  - Emotional and behavioural problems;
  - Experiencing debt;
  - Teenage pregnancy;
  - Needing medical treatment;
  - Leaving school/home when young;
  - Depressive symptoms;
  - Elevated levels of smoking, drinking and drug use during adolescence and adulthood.

- Figures from the Department for Work and Pensions show that 65% of 12- to 16-year-old children in low-income households do not live with both birth parents.

- A study published in the *Journal of Health and Social Behaviour* showed that the damage to health caused by divorce persists even after remarriage: 'among the currently married those who experienced one divorce or multiple disruptions show worse health on every dimension than the continuously married'.

- Divorce has been shown to be associated with a greater risk to men of heart attacks, strokes, cancer and dying earlier.
- A report from One plus One has also shown that adults who divorce have a greatly increased incidence (compared to those who remain married) of heart disease, cancer, alcoholism and suicide.

(www.christian.org.uk/theology/apologetics/marriage-and-family/divorce/)

Helpful Contacts/Resources

Help for victims of domestic abuse:

- National domestic abuse helpline (to find a refuge place): 0808 2000 247
- NCDV (to obtain an emergency injunction): https://www.ncdv.org.uk
- Women's Aid: https://womensaid.org.uk
- Police (reporting non-emergency): 101
- Drramona.com (resources – including safety plan, 'prayer wall')

Abortion information and support:

- CBRUK (Centre for Bio-ethical Reform UK): cbruk.org
- PASE (Post Abortion Support for Everyone): postabortsupport.org
- Brephos (helping churches respond to abortion): brephos.org

Challenging gender confusion:

- https://core-issues.org

Benefits and help with living costs:

- Entitled to (benefit calculator): www.entitledto.co.uk
- Universal Credit (payment to support with living costs): www.gov.uk/universal-credit

Housing and homeless advice:

- Local council: www.gov.uk/find-local-council
- Shelter (free housing advice): shelter.org.uk

Useful Books Expounding Scriptures on Marriage, Divorce and Remarriage

1. Andy Economides, *He Hates or GOD Hates* (Verité CM Ltd, 2021).
2. Barbara Roberts, *Not under Bondage: Biblical Divorce for Abuse, Adultery and Desertion* (Maschil Press, 2008).
3. Daniel R. Watson, 'Who Hates . . . Divorce? A Text-Critical Examination of Malachi 2:16 (*Midwestern Journal of Theology* 10. 1, 2011).
4. John MacArthur, *The Divorce Dilemma: God's Last Word on Lasting Commitment* (Day One Publications, 2009).

Other resources

1. Esther Sweetman, *Restored: A Handbook for Female Christian Survivors of Domestic Abuse* (Restored, 2019).

You can contact Hannah Nightingale:
diadem@livingstonesfellowship.uk